F ... ie

T0073403

Color is one of the most important tools in your visual storytelling toolbox. Kate explores all the essential aspects of color and provides a comprehensive guide for how aspiring and experienced data storytellers can use it more effectively.

—*Brent Dykes, author of* Effective Data Storytelling
and chief data storyteller at AnalyticsHero, LLC

Color is one of those things we often take for granted, especially when it comes to data. *ColorWise* opened my mind to the ways color can be used to greatly improve the storytelling impact of data visualizations.

—*Joe Reis, author of* Fundamentals of Data Engineering,
data engineer, and recovering data scientist

This book is a fun deep-dive into color theory and how the use of color can bring your data visualization to a whole new level. I love all the graphics and examples included in this book; it makes the learning fun and easy. I'd recommend this book to *any* data professional focusing on conveying convincing stories through data visualization. If you want your visualizations to really "pop" and stand out to your audience, the use of color (and this book) are for you.

—*Avery Smith, founder of Data Career Jumpstart*

Kate is an expert at shining a light on data storytelling. She is able to paint a vivid vision and bring light to shady details. Color is a powerful tool in data storytelling, but only if you use it wisely. This book will teach you how!

—*Gilbert Eijkelenboom, founder of MindSpeaking
and author of* People Skills for Analytical Thinkers

ColorWise

A Data Storyteller's Guide to the Intentional Use of Color

Kate Strachnyi

Beijing · Boston · Farnham · Sebastopol · Tokyo   O'REILLY®

ColorWise

by Kate Strachnyi

Published by O'Reilly Media, Inc., 1005 Gravenstein Highway North, Sebastopol, CA 95472.

O'Reilly books may be purchased for educational, business, or sales promotional use. Online editions are also available for most titles (*http://oreilly.com*). For more information, contact our corporate/institutional sales department: 800-998-9938 or *corporate@oreilly.com*.

Acquisitions Editor: Michelle Smith	**Proofreader:** Amnet Systems LLC
Devlopment Editor: Angela Rufino	**Indexer:** Potomac Indexing, LLC
Production Editor: Kate Galloway	**Interior Designer:** Monica Kamsvaag
Copyeditor: Charles Roumeliotis	**Cover Designer:** Susan Thompson
	Illustrator: Kate Dullea

November 2022:   First Edition

Revision History for the First Edition

2022-11-14:   First Release

See *http://oreilly.com/catalog/errata.csp?isbn=9781492097846* for release details.

978-1-492-09784-6

[LSI]

Contents

Preface

It's the day of the big interview for the job you've been after all your life. You wake up extra early, eat a healthy, energizing breakfast, take a 30-minute jog to get all your synapses firing, and take a hot shower to feel fully ready to conquer the world. You've got your clothes all laid out to impress the interview team with your sense of style and professionalism and head out the door in your bright red jacket, lime green pants, and neon purple shirt. Look out world, here you come (Figure P-1)!

Figure P-1. Mismatched outfit with a mix of colors

Cringeworthy, right? Unless the position you are interviewing for is a clown at the circus, those colors are not going to do the job today or any other day. We are extraordinarily cautious with the colors we choose to wear, the colors we paint our homes with, the colors we choose for our cars, even the colors we select for our oh-so-important smartphone cases!

Yet when it comes time to select colors for our infographics and data visualization creations, we often act like someone shook up a rainbow and spilled it all over the floor. Color is by far the most abused and neglected tool in data visualization. We abuse it by making color choices that make no sense, and we neglect it when we populate our hard work with software default settings, which are a good place to start but can be customized to suit your needs.

The lack of focus and commitment to color is a perplexing thing. When used correctly, color has no equal as a visualization tool—in advertising, in branding, in getting the message across to any audience you seek. Data analysts can make numbers dance and sing on command, but they sometimes struggle to create visually stimulating environments that convince the intended audience to tap their feet in time. Sales and marketing experts understand the customer's mindset, but often cannot seem to help from turning simple charts and graphs into a kaleidoscope of shades and hues that require a roadmap to figure out which side is up.

Fortunately, in the preceding example, we don't have to design our own fashions, although we do need to be responsible for being the best infographic tailors we can be to get color combinations that fit our purposes, engage our intended audiences, and draw the eye to the exact spot we want it to deliver the intended message every time.

Why I Wrote This Book

As founder of DATAcated, I see a staggering and frustrating amount of data visualizations where color is being poorly used on a weekly basis. Dozens of years ago when color was still a luxury on paper reports, and most businesses were still living in a black-and-white environment, misusing color wasn't the death knell that it is today. But with every business worth its salt the world over now fully embracing the digital revolution, real-time collaboration, and all of the bells and whistles that go with these advances, knowing how to use color appropriately has evolved from a nicety to a necessity.

We learn about color from an early age, but understanding how it connects our eyes to our brains and how the proper usage can transform graphics is an elusive subject for many. That's why I decided to undertake this book: to go on a mission to educate business and data professionals on the proper use of color.

The power of the internet and digital technology has clogged every industry and every niche with a glut of businesses all pursuing the same finite number of customers. That means companies need to scrape and claw for the type of differentiation that will elevate them away from the competition and crystalize why their offering is the best one on the market, whether that's for end-use customers, in business-to-business (B2B) relationships, or to promote their own projects inside the company environment.

How This Book Is Organized

This is a book that can be read in two ways. You can take it from beginning to end, creating a base of knowledge that starts at the broadest of foundations and builds upon that knowledge to define and refine very specific concepts of color as they relate to data visualization. Or, if you have experience in the field already, you can use this book as a reference guide that can greatly augment your existing skills when it comes to utilizing color correctly to represent data in graphs, charts, tables, and infographics. In doing so, you can learn more about not only the individual tips and tricks but also the theory behind them, why they work the way they do, and how to take the basics and augment them for your own future projects.

Regardless of which route you decide to take—and feel free to try both—this book will educate you on:

- The history, biology, and psychology of color theory
- Definitions of data visualization and data storytelling and color's vital role in both
- A myriad of rules and suggestions on how to select the best color scheme for your next data visualization
- How to appropriately address color vision deficiency to avoid alienating those without the full range of visual capabilities
- A closer consideration of color in cultural design
- Some common errors to avoid when using color in data visualization and storytelling

That list is just the tip of the iceberg. We're going to take a journey across time, various industries, and some fantastic case uses of color that depict both spectacular success and avoidable failure.

If you take away a few things from this text, I hope they include the following:

- Use color intentionally in everything you do. Don't just use the default settings in your data analysis or business intelligence software because you think it "knows best." As the data visualization designer, you possess the knowledge and power to use color intentionally to help tell your story.

- Be aware of color vision deficiency. It affects more people than you think and involves a whole host of conditions, not just what most people refer to as "color blindness." Strive to be as inclusive as possible.

- Take note of culture-laden connotations when selecting colors for your data visualization. The same color might be interpreted extremely differently across various cultures.

Who This Book Is For

The audience for this book includes data analysts, business analysts, data scientists, or anyone who has to deliver insights, design infographics and data visualizations, build dashboards, and tell data stories.

This book can be used as a reference when building data visualizations or as a teaching tool used to learn about proper use of color for data storytelling techniques and dashboarding.

Now that we've established the what, why, how, and who of this book, it's time to dig in and take a tour through our own history, biology, and psychology to understand how we process color, how it has been used over time, and what powerful, often subconscious effects it has on our minds.

O'Reilly Online Learning

O'REILLY® For more than 40 years, *O'Reilly Media* has provided technology and business training, knowledge, and insight to help companies succeed.

Our unique network of experts and innovators share their knowledge and expertise through books, articles, and our online learning platform. O'Reilly's online learning platform gives you on-demand access to live training courses, in-depth learning paths, interactive coding environments, and a vast collection of text and video from O'Reilly and 200+ other publishers. For more information, visit *https://oreilly.com*.

How to Contact Us

Please address comments and questions concerning this book to the publisher:

O'Reilly Media, Inc.

1005 Gravenstein Highway North

Sebastopol, CA 95472

800-998-9938 (in the United States or Canada)

707-829-0515 (international or local)

707-829-0104 (fax)

We have a web page for this book, where we list errata, examples, and supplemental information: *https://oreil.ly/colorwise*. You can also find additional information and resources at *https://www.datacated.com/colorwise*.

Email *bookquestions@oreilly.com* to comment or ask technical questions about this book.

For news and information about our books and courses, visit *https://oreilly.com*.

Find us on LinkedIn: *https://linkedin.com/company/oreilly-media*.

Follow us on Twitter: *https://twitter.com/oreillymedia*.

Watch us on YouTube: *https://youtube.com/oreillymedia*.

Acknowledgments

Thank you to the data community for the encouragement to take on the task of writing this book—your support is appreciated.

To Michelle Smith—thank you for taking a chance on the book idea and passing this on to the team at O'Reilly.

To my publisher (O'Reilly) and my editor (Angela Rufino), thank you for your guidance and feedback, and for helping me share the importance of being intentional with color when visualizing data. Thank you to Kate Galloway and Kristen Brown, who patiently helped prepare all of the book files and worked with me throughout production. I really appreciate the support from Charles Roumeliotis and Suzanne Huston, as well the illustrator, indexer, and everyone else involved in the process.

I'm grateful for all of the thought leaders in the data visualization space that have spent the time and effort researching the impact of color on data visualization and data storytelling. I've been inspired by many leaders in this space, including Cole Nussbaumer Knaflic, Edward Tufte, Alberto Cairo, David McCandless, and more. Special thanks goes out to those who took the time to review the book in its early stages and provided key feedback that helped shape the book. A shoutout to my early reviewers: Joe Reis, Jordan Morrow, Kimberly Herrington, Bernard Marr, Jon Schwabish, Brent Dykes, Mico Yuk, Bernard Marr, Avery Smith, Gilbert Eijkelenboom, and others.

A special thank-you goes out to Maureen Stone, digital color expert and former research scientist at Tableau, for providing extremely valuable feedback on several sections of the book. Maureen Stone is best known for her expertise in digital color and its applications, and has broad experience in digital design, interactive graphics, and user interface design.

Thank you to my family for your support throughout this process. Special thanks to my two daughters and husband who provided feedback on the images that we included in the book. I'd also love to acknowledge the support from my mother, who has always been there to help with anything that was necessary.

Color Theory and History

Mention the word "color" and most people's minds explode into their favorite sights and memories. The deep blue of the ocean. Shades of green in a lush forest. The perfectly balanced blend of brown-and-white in a chocolate-vanilla ice cream sundae. The golden hues of sunlight bursting through the clouds on a stormy day (Figure 1-1).

Figure 1-1. Four images showing a view of the ocean, a forest, a chocolate-vanilla sundae, and sun shining through clouds

In this chapter, we will define "color" and take a brief walk through history to discuss its evolution through time. You'll learn about how humans biologically see color, including an introduction to color theory and color psychology.

So What Is Color?

Color is the aspect of things that is caused by differing qualities of light being reflected or emitted by them. You need light to see color. When light hits an object, some colors bounce off the object and some are absorbed by the object.

Back in the 1660s, Sir Isaac Newton did more to contribute to science than letting an apple pop him in the head; he also started experimenting with prisms and sunlight, showing that the clear white light that made up everything people could see outside was actually composed of seven visible colors—the scientific establishment of the visible spectrum (Figure 1-2).

Figure 1-2. Isaac Newton experimenting with prisms and sunlight

Newton's work was the progenitor for a massive number of breakthroughs in chemistry, optics, physics, the study of color in nature, and how perception works. His studies were predated by others going back thousands of years to the time of Aristotle in ancient Greece, who postulated that God sent celestial rays of light from heaven; he believed all colors originated from white and black—the visual representations of lightness and darkness—and that they were directly related to the four earthly elements of fire, earth, air, and water. These beliefs were widely held until Newton's time.

Newton posed his theories in his work *Opticks*, which has been slightly modified in spelling over time, but remains a commonly used business phrase into the 21st century. He revolutionized the idea of light being only one color by writing, "[I]f the Sun's Light consisted of but one sort of Rays, there would be but one Colour in the whole World..."

Newton identified the colors inside the prism that would become the acronym learned the world over by school children as ROY G BIV (red, orange, yellow, green, blue, indigo, and violet) (Figure 1-3).

Figure 1-3. Prism colors—red, orange, yellow, green, blue, indigo, and violet

The visible spectrum is the part of the electromagnetic spectrum that can be seen by the human eye (Figure 1-4). There are seven parts of the electromagnetic spectrum:

Radio waves

The lowest range, used for communications including voice, entertainment media, and data.

Microwaves

The second lowest, used for radar, high-bandwidth communications, and as a heat source in industrial applications and consumer and commercial microwave ovens.

Infrared

The range between microwave and visible light. Humans can feel it as heat if it is intense enough, but cannot see it. Animals such as frogs, snakes, fish, and mosquitos rely on it for their vision.

Visible light

Right in the middle of the electromagnetic spectrum, these are the wavelengths visible to most, but not all human eyes.

Ultraviolet

Falls between visible light and X-rays and is a component of sunlight invisible to the human eye. It has multiple uses in medicine and industry, but also causes skin cancer in large doses.

X-rays

There are actually two types of X-rays, designated as "soft" and "hard," that have different spots on the spectrum. Soft X-rays are between ultraviolet and gamma rays, while hard X-rays are in the same region as gamma rays.

Gamma rays

Mostly known throughout the world as the stuff that turned Bruce Banner into the Incredible Hulk, it does in fact cause damage to living tissue, but in small doses can be used to kill cancer cells. In large amounts, it is very dangerous, and even fatal to humans.

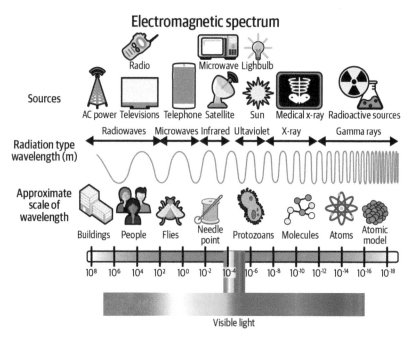

Figure 1-4. Electromagnetic spectrum from various sources, along with radiation type and approximate scale of wavelength

Newton further shook up previously held beliefs when he revealed that color does not inherently exist in objects, but rather the surface of an object reflects certain colors and absorbs the rest. Only the colors that get reflected are the ones that we see, and thus the ones that define the color of an object. Therefore, a ripe banana sitting on your kitchen counter is not yellow because yellow is part of a banana's characteristics, but because the surface of its peels reflects the wavelengths that our eyes and brains translate into "yellow" and absorbs the rest. Thus, an all-white object like a sheet of printer paper reflects all visible wavelengths of color and a freshly laid tar designed to fix a pothole appears black because it absorbs all of the wavelengths.

Red, green, and blue (RGB) are known as the additive primary colors in the spectrum. There are many sets of RGB values, each producing part of the visible color spectrum. When these three are combined in balanced amounts, they make pure white. By varying the amount of the three of them, all other colors on the spectrum can be produced.

How Do We See Color?

The process of seeing color starts in the retina, which is physically part of the eye, but considered to be part of the brain (Figure 1-5). It is covered by millions upon millions of light-sensitive cells called rods and cones based on their similarities to those shapes. These cells act as receptors that process the incoming light into nerve impulses and send them via the optic nerve to the cortex inside the brain.

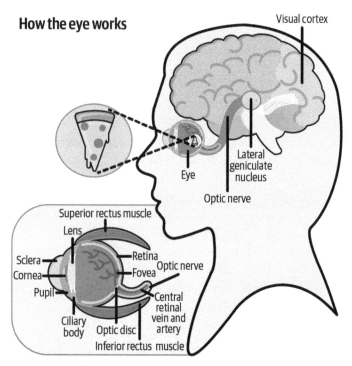

How the eye works

Figure 1-5. Demonstration of how the human brain perceives color

The rods are found in the highest concentration around the edge of the retina, with more than 120 million found in each eye (Figure 1-6). The rods are useful for low-light vision. The cones are responsible for luminance, which is the grayscale part of color.

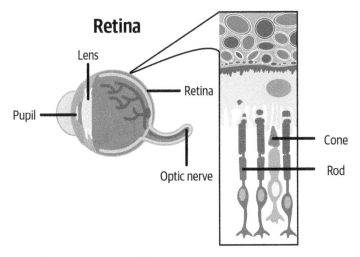

Figure 1-6. The cellular organization of the retina[1]

Cones, meanwhile, are most frequent in the middle of your retinas, and diminish in number toward the periphery. There are about six million cones in each eye transmitting the more intense levels of light, which translate into colors and visual sharpness. The cones come in three different types: long, medium, and short, which are sensitive to long, medium, and short wavelengths of light. When they work in harmony, they supply the brain with ample interpretation to identify colors and interpret them as well, key tasks for data visualization and storytelling (Figure 1-7).

---

1 Image adapted from Cleveland Clinic (*https://oreil.ly/NS3yr*).

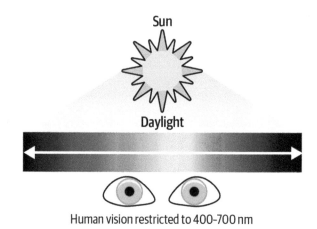

Figure 1-7. *Visible light wavelengths impact the eyeball and are interpreted by the brain*

The optic nerve connects to the thalamus, sort of a central hub for all kinds of signals coming into our brains from our senses. The thalamus takes these signals and processes them, determining what is necessary and what isn't. It also combines and repackages what it receives with new information from elsewhere and sends that information to other parts of the brain for further use. In data visualization, color can be used as both signal and noise. We'll discuss in future sections how to avoid using color as noise and focus on using it as a signal for important insights.

The next stop is the visual cortex, located at the back of the brain (Figure 1-8). There are different types of cells located here that break down the information being sent by the thalamus. Some of the cells identify what shape an object is, while others note what color it is, what texture it appears to be, and whether it is moving or not. All of the signals combine to form the entire image. This construct moves on to the prefrontal cortex, located above the eyes and behind the forehead, where the brain combines and processes multiple types of information from the senses, along with emotions and memories, to produce not only a total picture of the item, but what we know and/or believe about that object from prior experiences and learned knowledge.

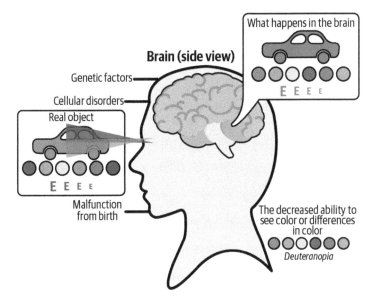

Figure 1-8. How the eye works when viewing an object

Let's take an example that could easily be a case of mistaken identity. You're walking down the street on a brisk evening jaunt and you pause when you notice something coiled up in a neighbor's yard a couple of doors down (Figure 1-9). The light is receding as the sun sets and it's costing you the ability to see much beyond the object's shape and size. Long and wrapped around itself multiple times, it gives your brain two immediate options—it could be a garden hose that hasn't been properly put up after being used, or it could be a snake lying in wait for its next dinner to saunter by.

Only when you get closer can you see either the bright green of the hose or the organic textured brown-black of a snake's skin. The bright green color of the hose triggers information in your brain that designates the hose as harmless and maybe calls up images of plants getting watered or you as a child racing through a sprinkler on a hot summer day. If you see the darker color and slimy look instead, your brain will trigger danger signals and emotions of fear and the need to retreat to safety will emerge.

Figure 1-9. Long green garden hose laying on a lawn that looks like a snake

What Is Color Theory?

Color theory blends the science and art of color and details how we perceive color, and how colors mix, match, and contrast with one another. It also involves how colors influence the messages we communicate to one another. To understand how color theory works, put yourself at your local grocery store in your mind's eye. When you turn down the aisle for soft drinks, you know you want to buy a case of Coca-Cola Classic (Figure 1-10).

Figure 1-10. Cans of Coca-Cola and other soda bottles on display in a supermarket

Despite the fact that there are hundreds of selections lining the shelves from the floor to several feet above your head, it only takes you a moment or two to identify a case of Coke from all the rest and set it in your basket. Did you look at the label on each and every item to find out where they keep the Coke? Of course not! Instead, you headed straight for the tell-tale red box, the color of which I suspect you can call up in your mind right now, and the white script lettering that goes along with it. This is the power of color theory and why color is so vital to things like product branding.

Note

Most people will decide within 90 seconds if they like a product or not, and 90% of that decision is based solely on the color of the packaging.[2]

As mentioned earlier, red, green, and blue combine to form the additive color mixing model. Televisions and movie projectors use these primary colors to create the rest when they broadcast a show or a movie (Figure 1-11).

A second model is the subtractive color mixing model, composed of the colors cyan, magenta, yellow, and black (CMYK). This model is used for colors on physical surfaces like packaging, signage, and paper. Newspapers use them when printing color editions or using color advertising. It's known as the subtractive model because adding more color subtracts more light from the paper. CMYK is the better model for printing things out.

---

2 Cecile Jordan, "Color Psychology: How Color Influences Opinions About Your Brand," Beyond Definition, July 22, 2021, *https://oreil.ly/eUyYt*.

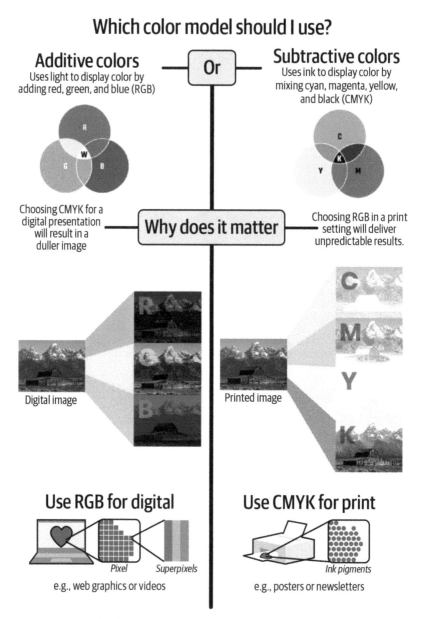

Figure 1-11. Additive and subtractive color models and when to use each one

Color theory can be represented by the color wheel (Figure 1-12), which breaks colors into three categories:

- Primary colors
- Secondary colors
- Tertiary colors

We have our old friend Isaac Newton to thank for the color wheel. He documented the first one, which is used today by artists and designers the world over in an amazing array of ways. The primary colors on the wheel are red, yellow, and blue. The secondary colors—those created when the primary colors are mixed together—include purple, orange, and green. There are six additional tertiary colors, which are created by mixing primary and secondary colors together to get combinations like red-violet or blue-green.

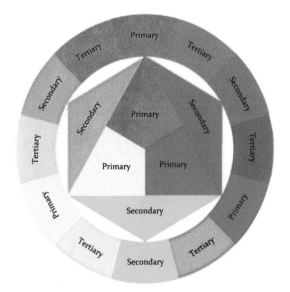

Figure 1-12. Color wheel that demonstrates the primary, secondary, and tertiary colors

Drawing a line down the center of the color wheels also distinguishes between the warm colors (red, orange, yellow) and the cool colors (blue, green, purple). Warm and cool associate colors with different temperatures, which are essential in creating advertising, branding, and data visualization for different audiences. Warm colors create sensations of action, brightness, and energy.

Remember that case of Cokes you spotted in just a few seconds at the grocery store? In the Western world, red is proven to be a color that promotes excitability and stimulates appetites in most people. When your cones feed that bright Coca-Cola red into your brain, it can trigger thoughts, emotions, and memories of things like hot summer days, a cold glass in your hand, the sound of the "fizz" when you pour a drink over ice, and so on. Cool colors, on the other hand, such as blue, purple, and green, are often identified with feelings of calm, peace, serenity, and trust in the Western world. Next time you're watching TV, try to count the number of car companies and healthcare companies using blue in their logos; you might need a calculator to add them all up!

When you are looking to make a pair of colors stand out by using them at the same time, you can select a warm color and a cool color together. These pairs are called contrasting colors, or in some disciplines, complementary colors. Two colors that appear on opposite sides of the color wheel are often thought of as clashing with one another, but matching them up often results in very pleasing contrasts.

For instance, red and green are contrasting colors that appear on opposite ends of the color wheel, but few people complain about seeing them together on Christmas wrapping paper (Figure 1-13)! The more transitional colors there are between a pair of colors, the greater the contrast between them.

Figure 1-13. Green- and red-colored Christmas wrapping paper

Other well-used combinations include analogous colors, which sit right next to each other on a color wheel, such as blue and purple, or orange, red, and yellow. In an analogous color scheme, one color will dominate, another will support the first, and the third will provide small accents.

Triadic colors are usually a trio that are evenly spaced around the color wheel to give a lot of contrast. International fast-food chain Burger King is a well-known example of this, mixing its red lettering inside the orange "burger bun" with a blue circle wrapped around both (Figure 1-14).

Figure 1-14. Burger King logo

Hues, Shades, Tints, and Tones

Seeing how there are only 12 colors on the color wheel we just discussed, your childhood self might be wondering how in the world that short supply translates into the set of 64 crayons (Figure 1-15) we all loved as kids (and many of us continue to use as adults).

Figure 1-15. Open box of 64 crayons with a few crayons out of the box

You know what I'm talking about—for every standard blue, red, or yellow, you've also got periwinkle, cornflower, sea green, and my personal favorite— neon carrot. The variations come from hues, shades, tints, and tones, four terms that get horribly mixed up and interchanged by people—both amateurs and professionals—who have no idea what any of them actually mean. Let's break all four of them down so that you never confuse one for another again.

HUES

Hues are easiest to remember, because they are simply the pure colors that appear on the color wheel. Those are the primary, secondary, and tertiary colors. Hues do not include black or white. When a hue is altered by adding black, white, or both to it, it ceases to be a hue and becomes something else. So, the next time someone tells you that they want to change a color to a slightly lighter hue, remind them that they don't know what they're talking about, or at least be smug in your own mind that they don't.

SHADES

Shades are created when black is added to a hue, producing richer, darker, and more intense colors. It's easy to remember that shade means adding black to it if you consider the origin of the word "shade" in mythology. In Greek mythology, shades were spirits living in shadow in the underworld dominion of Hades. They were perpetually in darkness. Mixing black into other colors can be a difficult task because black tends to change hues quickly, even if only a small amount is used. Sometimes, other dark hues like purple and blue are added to brighter colors in place of or in addition to black to make the mix more palatable.

TINTS

Tints appear when white is added to a hue on the color wheel. The addition of white makes any color less intense, desaturating it in the process. Tints are often referred to as pastel colors—particularly when red is desaturated into pink and blue is considerably lightened. These lighter colors often generate emotions of calm and quiet.

TONES

Tones are the result of adding both black and white to a hue—which is roughly the equivalent of adding gray. The mixture of black and white can send hues in a number of directions; they can be darker or lighter than their original incarnation, less saturated, or more intense. Tones often emulate the colors we see in the natural world better than hues, tints, or shades because they often have complex qualities that are reflective of the way that items in nature are affected by age, light, and weather.

Here is a visual that helps explain the four concepts with the color yellow; observe the differences between the pure hue, tints, shades, and tones (Figure 1-16).

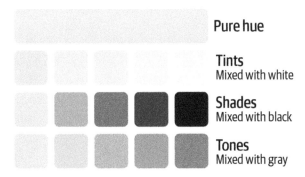

Pure hue

Tints
Mixed with white

Shades
Mixed with black

Tones
Mixed with gray

Figure 1-16. Demonstration of the difference between hues, tints, shades, and tones

The Psychology of Color

We've danced a few times throughout this chapter on particular emotions and feelings that different colors create. There is a clear connection between our feelings, moods, and behaviors and different colors. Certain colors are even associated with physiological reactions such as eyestrain, higher blood pressure, and faster metabolism. How does color psychology work in general? Some of what people perceive when they see colors is inextricably tied to the culture they hail from. This is a topic we'll explore further in the book. Here, we can break down the most well-known and well-used colors in the world and see the different emotions they often conjure up and the symbolism that we tend to associate with them at first sight.

BLACK

Black is not on the color wheel and isn't actually considered a color in technical terms; it's the absorption of all colors. That said, it is very commonly used in multiple forms of visualization and is considered a color in the design sense. It has one of the widest ranges of emotions tied to it, giving perceptions of power, mystery, luxury, boldness, and unhappiness. Car companies often use it to promote elegance and sophistication, the kind of emotions you get when you see couples in black dresses and tuxedos headed to a classy party. Of course, in many cultures, black is the color of death, fear, and all things evil. Considering the audience you're using when black comes into play is very important, especially if you are crossing cultural lines.

WHITE

Much like black, white does not appear on the color wheel but is still considered a color in the design sense. Objects look white when they reflect all the visible light in the environment, which varies. Also, much like black, white's meaning can change dramatically depending on which culture you are using it in. In Western cultures, white means purity, peacefulness, and cleanliness. It's frequently seen on wedding dresses, in hospital corridors, and in church paintings of angels and heaven. In Eastern cultures, it has the polar opposite meaning, being tied to funerals and mourning rituals, and associated with sadness and death. It can also give negative emotions of cold, isolation, and starkness, such as an empty room. On the positive side, that can translate into freshness, simplicity, and cleanliness, all nice qualities when designing something and being comfortable with the use of white space.

RED

We've touched on red a time or two in our discussion. The more you look around outside, the more you'll realize that it's not just the leading beverage in the world that is addicted to red, but scores of makers of food and drink. The reason? Red is known to be a color that increases your appetite. When you're driving down the road and see a McDonald's, Chick-fil-A, Wendy's, or Sonic, you'll notice there's plenty of red on the signs. That's to get your brain talking to your stomach about the fact that a giant hamburger and a side of fries is probably the best thing in the world for you right now. Research finds that red provokes the strongest emotions of any color out there. It is used to create feelings of power, anger, passion, and love in different circumstances. Red symbolizes danger and caution, which is why it is used for stop signs and traffic lights, along with other cautionary traffic signals in Western cultures. In Eastern cultures, red is often celebrated and considered a positive color. But it also is a color that is meant to stimulate buyers with excitement and passion for products. It is one of the colors that can stimulate physical responses in people, including an uptick in respiration, heart rate, and blood pressure. It also is associated with aggression and dominance.[3] In data visualizations, red is often used as an alert that something bad has happened; this is more common in North America.

BLUE

Generally considered the most popular color in the world—blue has ties to calmness and serenity that touch on its natural association with water. It is seen as conservative and traditional, and as a sign of both reliability and stability. However, the term "feeling blue" goes against all of these characteristics and can create feelings of sadness and aloofness, as showcased with legendary painter Pablo Picasso during his "blue period."

GREEN

Few colors are more associated with nature than green, which calls to life images of your childhood backyard, wide meadows, and lush forests. It is often described as being both refreshing and tranquil. Green is considered a cool color because it has shorter wavelengths. Particularly in the last few decades, it has also been tied to feelings of health and products that are organic, creative, or environmentally

---

3 Kendra Cherry, "The Color Psychology of Red," Verywell Mind, last updated September 13, 2020, https://oreil.ly/LhP5A.

friendly. Of course, in the United States, green is also irrevocably tied to money and wealth since it is the color of US currency. That doesn't always translate to foreign audiences, however.

YELLOW

Yellow is bright, intense, and quickly grabs attention, but it can also lead to visual fatigue if it is used too long or too much. Most people associate it with brightness and warmth because of its connection to the sun and sunlight. However, of the most-used colors, it is considered to generate the most eye fatigue. Using it as a background for computer monitors or on paper can lead to eyestrain. At its best, yellow works well to stimulate positive feelings—like when someone sees the golden arches of McDonald's off in the distance and knows that grumbling in their stomach can soon be quelled. It is also known to increase metabolism,[4] but in large amounts, such as a room painted yellow, it can also result in more frustration and anger. It is recommended to use yellow to promote purchases; the eyes see yellow first, and with so many other distractions in retail stores, you need to capture your customer's attention quickly.

PURPLE

Purple is rather unique among the colors in that it is used less frequently than most but tends to be viewed as majestic, mysterious, imaginative, and intriguing—with few negatives in its ledger. The origin of purple as a royal, regal color dates all the way back to ancient times when Phoenician purple dye was affordable only by the aristocracy of the day; it was quite rare and extremely expensive. Its legacy has endured for millennia, to the point of royal purple being a well-known derivative. In both Virgil's *Aeneid* and Homer's *Iliad*, Alexander the Great and the ancient kings of Egypt are depicted as dressing in purple robes. In more recent times, the late Queen Elizabeth II wore purple following her coronation in 1953. Purple is also associated with wisdom, spirituality, and bravery, although in parts of Europe, it is used to symbolize mourning and death as well. In the US military, the Purple Heart is one of the highest honors a soldier can have awarded, symbolizing bravery and courage. Its history dates back to George Washington, who created the Badge of Military Merit in 1782.

---

4 Kendra Cherry, "The Color Psychology of Yellow," Verywell Mind, last updated May 11, 2022, *https://oreil.ly/v79J0*.

BROWN

While most people find this color oddly unappealing, brown has its uses across the board. Its concept of the woods invokes ideas of strength, security, and nature, but on the flip side, those come with isolation, sadness, and loneliness. There are plenty of popular brands that turn to brown for their marketing, including the world-famous UPS, along with a couple that will get your stomach churning—M&Ms and Hershey's.

ORANGE

Like yellow, orange can be way overused with people growing to hate it when it's everywhere. At its best, it is energetic, innovative, and enthusiastic, and often used with new businesses that are hoping to stand out as well as in tropical settings where sunshine and happiness are the staple of the day. Since orange is a secondary color born of red and yellow, it tends to symbolize a lot of excitement and enthusiasm. It also has quite a bit of range, given that it is tied to the autumn season with leaves changing colors, pumpkins, and Halloween, but also to healthy spring and summer feelings and events like fresh citrus fruits and sunsets.

PINK

Although gender roles are continuously being redefined in the 21st century, most people associate pink with all things girly and female, including love, kindness, and romance. Pink in a room usually means there's a baby on the way, and can symbolize nurturing and calming effects. This has even been used as a reverse psychology effect, where sports teams will paint the visitors' locker room pink to throw their opponents off their naturally aggressive, confident frame of mind![5] Being joyful and creative are also states of mind that revolve around pink.

GRAY

Gray is useful in data visualizations as it can be used for all of the supporting details; this also helps the colors of your more important elements stand out and makes it easier for the reader to distinguish what is important. An example of supporting details can be the axis, tick marks, less important annotations, or simply data points that are not conveying the key message. In the Christian religion, gray is the color of ashes and can be interpreted as a biblical symbol of mourning

---

5 Kabir Chibber, "Sports Teams Think the Color Pink Can Help Them Win," *Quartz*, August 28, 2018, *https://oreil.ly/qawAg*.

and repentance. It is also the color worn by monks and represents modesty and humility. Gray is also linked in many cultures with the elderly because of the association with gray hair.

Why People Don't Always See the Same Color

One of the biggest viral phenomena of the last decade occurred in 2015 when a photograph of a dress appeared on social media accompanied by the question of whether the two-tone apparel was black and blue or white and gold (Figure 1-17). It seemed like a bizarre question to just about anyone who looked at the photo, but more bizarre still were the looks on people's faces when their friends, family members, and coworkers glanced at the photo and saw a garment with completely different colors than they themselves registered. The dress was bought by the mother of a bride-to-be on the small island of Colonsay, Scotland. When she posted it on her Facebook page, a considerable debate ensued among other members of the wedding party, then the whole island, then seemingly the whole world! Within a day, the debate had been written up on Buzzfeed in an article that generated 673,000 views, and a *Wired* article rang up 32.8 million unique visitors. When popular singer Taylor Swift commented on it, her Tweet was liked 154,000 times and retweeted 111,000 times.

Figure 1-17. A dress that appears to be different colors—white and gold or black and blue

So, which was it? Well, when the wedding occurred, the dress turned out to be blue and black, which baffled some wedding goers and did the same for many across the internet. Bevil Conway, a neuroscientist from Wellesley College who studies vision and color, said the discrepancy came from the visual system trying to discount the chromatic bias. Some people discounted the blue side and saw the dress as white and gold, while others discounted the gold side and saw blue and black.

It happens more often than you think, and some of the problem is with a feature that photo editors and photographers use called *white balance* in which color casts are removed from an object that is physically white, so it remains white in the picture. White balancing shifts all the colors, not just the white objects. A more biological reason is that people have differences in their color vision that has them seeing different tints, shades, and tones when presented with an object. This leads to confusion where both sides think they are right and are baffled when people claim to see something that completely goes against what their own eyes are telling them.

There are other reasons why people don't see the same color—this is related to color vision deficiency, or "color blindness," a topic we will cover in a later chapter.

Summary

This chapter covered some important concepts around how we see color. Next, we'll discuss how to intentionally use color for data storytelling. We will use what we've learned about color theory and color psychology to design effective data visualizations.

2

Data Visualization and Data Storytelling

Like so many other revolutions before it, data is a great teacher, with the ability to transfer information from the ephemeral to the tangible with powerful results. Data is defined as factual information (such as measurements or statistics) used as a basis for reasoning, discussion, or calculation. Additionally, we can define data as information in digital form that can be transmitted or processed.[1]

Data becomes more useful once it's transformed into a data visualization or used in a data story. Data storytelling is the ability to effectively communicate insights from a dataset using narratives and visualizations. It can be used to put data insights into context and inspire action from your audience. Color can be very helpful when you are trying to make information stand out within your data visualizations.

In data storytelling, color helps to set the tone and enforces a unique message for the underlying visualizations. Color aids in developing a specific atmosphere that can convert a data visualization into an emotion-packed data story.

In this chapter, we will discuss the concept of data visualization, exploring different methods for portraying data such as time series, frequency, relationships, networks, and more. You'll learn about data storytelling and the types of colors that can be used to deliver insights (i.e., diverging, sequential, categorical).

What Is Data Visualization?

Data visualization is the practice of taking insights found in data analysis and turning them into numbers, graphs, charts, and other visual concepts to make

---

1 *Merriam-Webster, "Data," https://oreil.ly/cH1YK.*

them easier to grasp, understand, learn from, and utilize. It is the graphic representation of data, the ability to snapshot what has been collected, learned, and revealed, so that it can be harnessed and utilized not just in the moment it is revealed, but in the future term as well.

The visualization of data can be thought of as both a science and an art in that the way it is displayed is often as important to its understanding as the actual information that is being displayed. At its very best, it takes complex data sets that have been compiled over different time intervals and turns them into visual representations that are much easier to understand, commit to memory, and adopt into future practices.

Let's review an example of how data visualization is easier to interpret than data in its raw form. Take a look at Figure 2-1. The data on the left (table) and the data on the right (line graph) is the same; however, the data within the line graph makes it easy to follow the trends of inbound leads month to month and see the dip in inbound leads in April as well as the surge in May.

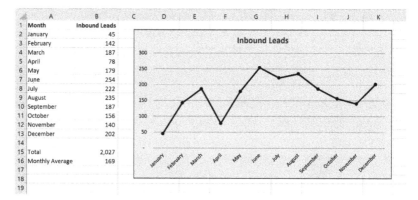

Figure 2-1. A table and graph that shows monthly inbound leads for 2019

History tells us that the Ishango bone (Figure 2-2) is not just the first use of recorded data in history, but also the first look at data visualization. In 1960, archeologists in what is now Uganda made a startling discovery while sifting through artifacts from a prehistoric site of Paleolithic tribes. A tally stick that later was named the Ishango bone showed notches placed on it that scientists believe were used to count the number of supplies a tribe had or how much it had to trade with other tribes of a certain resource. The calculations performed here were nothing more than simple addition, but having those numbers in hand let them make assumptions about how much food they had in storage for the future and how much they could afford to trade.[2]

Ishango bone

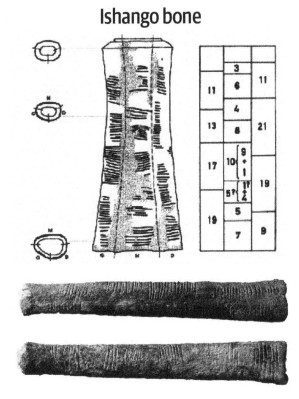

Figure 2-2. Ishango bone that was used as a tally stick for calculations in prehistoric times

Theirs was a technique that is still practiced by every farmer, rancher, and businessperson who deals in a natural or manmade resource today, placing the "birthdate" of data collection and visualization at around 20,000 BC.[3] The natives who scratched or carved their supply tallies into these bones and sticks were doing so not just to take count in the moment, but to have a reference point to return to and utilize in the future.

---

2 Anne Hauzuer, "Ishango Bone," in *Encyclopaedia of the History of Science, Technology, and Medicine in Non-Western Cultures*, Springer, 2008, *https://oreil.ly/UFH3A*.

3 "Prehistoric Math," Story of Mathematics, *https://oreil.ly/Z9f6O*.

In terms of human achievement and brain power, it is one of the most overlooked and underappreciated developments in history—not living in the moment, concerned only with the next need for fire, the next hunger pangs, the next quenching of the thirst, but instead focused on planning for what's coming next, trying to make an uncertain future more predictable by the use of data and planning.

Throughout history, some of the greatest leaps forward in human understanding have come as a result of data visualization. Claudius Ptolemy created a map projection of the earth (Figure 2-3) as a sphere with latitude and longitude lines in the second century that remained a standard reference throughout the world for more than 1,200 years.

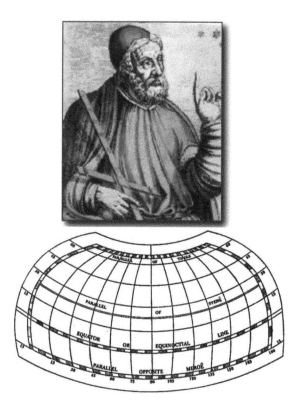

Figure 2-3. Map projection of the earth (created by Claudius Ptolemy)[4]

---

4 Image credits: Rachel Quist, "Ptolemy's Geographia," Geography Realm, November 30, 2011, *https://oreil.ly/9otCt*; #119 Ptolemy, *https://oreil.ly/0cHRi*.

Rene Descartes cocreated the idea of a two-dimensional coordinate system as well as analytic geometry that heavily influenced how most charts and graphs look today.[5] Pierre de Fermat and Blaine Pascal combined to push this work forward through the use of statistics and probability theory that are the very foundation of how we conceptualize data in the modern world.[6] According to data scientists, the current amount of data produced is 2.5 quintillion bytes of data per day.[7] That's 2,500,000,000,000,000,000 if you're scoring at home. Figure 2-4 demonstrates the amount of data we create and notes that 90% of the world's data today has been created in the last two years alone! To help you visualize this, imagine filling 10 million Blu-ray discs with data. If you stack those discs on top of each other, this would end up being the height of four Eiffel Towers!

Every day we create 2,500,000,000,000,000,000
(2.5 quintillion) bytes of data
This would fill ten million blu-ray disks, the height of which stacked
would measure the height of four Eiffel Towers on top of one another.

90% of the world's
data today has been
created in the last
two years alone

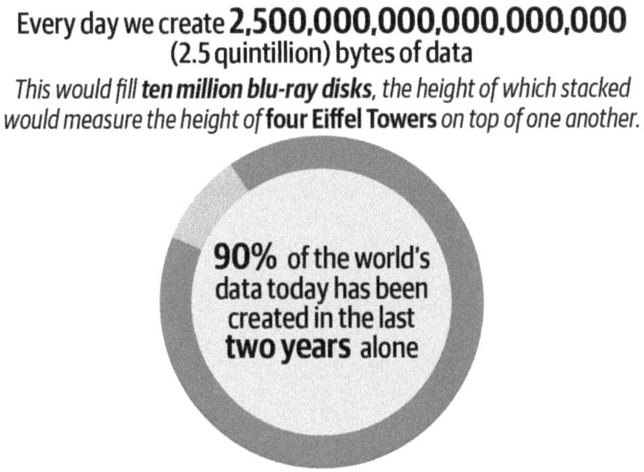

Figure 2-4. The vast amount of data we create on a daily basis[8]

---

5 "Rene Descartes and the Fly on the Ceiling," Wild Maths, last accessed November 7, 2022, *https://oreil.ly/7a1Q6*.

6 "Probability Theory / Blaise Pascal / Pierre de Fermat," *https://oreil.ly/8PGTM*.

7 Eric Griffith, "90 Percent of the Big Data We Generate Is an Unstructured Mess," *PCMag*, November 15, 2018, *https://oreil.ly/qlv08*.

8 Image credit: Griffith, "90 Percent of the Big Data We Generate Is an Unstructured Mess."

Deriving Meaning from Data

Especially when working with large data sets, visualization is entirely necessary for data to be put to use by anyone past data scientists. Without this medium for understanding, it becomes impossible to quantify, impossible to put into practical use, and by the time it could be explained through some other format, it would already be outdated.

In business use and beyond, the most valuable component of data analysis is the ability to identify trends and patterns, visualize them, and use them to change behaviors and plan for the future. As data has become more commonplace and data sets begin to stretch the breadth of human comprehension, being able to accurately visualize and understand data has become an absolutely essential component of every business.

Even data analysts themselves are not always able to grasp the meaning and see the revelation involved from the process of analysis without the use of visual stimulus. Processes such as machine learning (ML) and other forms of artificial intelligence (AI) can actively find trends and turn them into insights to be implemented. However, if the human component of this equation cannot grasp what is being seen and what can be done about it, none of it bears any relevance.

Our machines are helpers, not decision makers. Their insights are not the final word in the discussion, merely the work of our most nimble observers who can ramp up time spent on analysis by factors that our counterparts even a generation ago would have a hard time believing. In statistics classes, we are taught to be able to read raw numbers and gain insight from them. Seeing patterns on a spreadsheet or an Excel table takes skill, but it is doable, and even essential to get an early grasp of what trends and patterns look like.

For someone wishing to go into data analysis as a profession, it is and should be a required skill, just like someone learning photography should start on a film camera and learn to develop negatives in a dark room to understand what the basic process looks like and how things come together to form the modern use of the technical skill. However, understanding the process is not required by everyone. A great photographer does not ask the editor of their magazine to venture into the dark room with them anymore and look at a single image with a magnifying glass under a red light to approve of a single image; they use digital cameras and transmit images by text or email for approval in seconds.

Similarly, data analysts and scientists aren't going to dump 50 pages of printer paper onto the desk of the CFO of their corporation and ask her to sift through the raw data to identify trends. For example, we can't expect that the CFO will be able to identify the trend of a certain product no longer selling well so that she can then deduce that it should be taken out of the company's normal rotation of stock. Instead, they will take the raw data and construct a graph, chart, or other visual representation that lets the C-suite level leaders easily see the reduction in sales over the course of a few months or a year compared with the increase of other items to establish the pattern that forms the insight into what should be done next.

In the business world, understanding is the great equalizer so that everyone in a company that is a key stakeholder or decision maker can be on the same page and look at issues through the same lens.

Speaking the Same Language

One of the most debilitating things in business is that different teams often feel like they are trying to communicate in foreign languages to other teams, and to the management of their company. The sales department has a term for all of its metrics, advertising a second, logistics a third, and accounting yet another. This breakdown in communication can have enormous consequences that are not even realized at the moment. Trends that have tremendous significance to your research and development department might not register as such to sales and marketing, and vice versa.

The common language in all of these arenas is data—numbers that cannot be misrepresented by different choices of terms. Carefully designed charts and graphs and other representations break down communication barriers and ensure that the true meaning of the data is on display to be grasped by everyone present.

Power of Visualizing Data

What are the advantages of understanding data and being able to visualize it? It starts with the obvious: our eyes are naturally drawn to colors and patterns. One need only look at the standard children's toy or educational aid to grasp that from the moment we arrive in this world, we are drawn to these concepts.

Our eyes filter information quickly to our brains as we see different representations of color, different lines symbolizing different meanings, and so forth. Not only do we quickly grasp the patterns, but we more readily grasp the outliers.

When we see a pie chart (Figure 2-5) of contributions to our annual fundraising event with three fairly equal slices but one tiny sliver representing donations from the local chamber of commerce, you can bet that every time we see the chamber's emblem somewhere or speak to one of its members, our brains will immediately flash to that tiny sliver of donation failure.

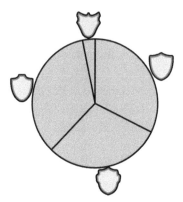

Figure 2-5. Pie chart of annual fundraising contributions

Every set of data tells a story, but when you utilize the power of visualization, that story has a purpose that is known to all who view it.

Note

Data visualization has the power of unity, to put everyone on the same page and in the same frame of mind when collaborating, whether it's in the conference room, the boardroom, or over a virtual video call.

Visualizations can remove the background noise from enormous sets of data so that only the most important points stand out to the intended audience. This is particularly important in the era of big data. The more data there is, the more chance for noise and outliers to interfere with the core concepts of the data set.

Sometimes, the simple pie charts and bar graphs we all learned as school children are not always the best representation for the complex concepts we are seeking to simplify in the business world. That's one of the reasons we refer to data visualization as both an art and a science. Visual designers need to be able to use the proper form and format to harness the data they are sharing to make it palatable to their target audience and also truly represent what the point of this data set is. Being too simple and boring is just as much of a risk as a visualization that is too complex and technical. Keep in mind though that unless you know how to properly design complex data visualizations, the best advice is to keep it simple.

What Is Data Storytelling?

Data storytelling is an effective way to get your team and your users the answers they need with a minimum amount of time and effort committed on their part. The more digital everything gets, the more dashboards, spreadsheets, and other business intelligence tools come trickling down from on high. The problem that results from having all these forms of interpretation is that while dashboards and spreadsheets are great at telling you what happened, they're not nearly as good at telling you why it happened.

In short, the need for human intervention in manual reporting and data wrangling slows down the process of communicating what data is finding in an organization.

While there are numerous great tools capable of presenting data in tables and charts, they lack the extremely important component of a narrative that can more effectively and efficiently communicate both information and key insights.

Data storytelling is a method of communicating information that is custom-fit for a specific audience and offers a compelling narrative to prove a point, highlight a trend, make a sale, or all of the above. Sharing stories to share information is a human tradition that dates back as far as our distant ancestors gathered around a fire or painting pictures on cave walls.

Plenty of scientific evidence exists that shows storytelling as the primary form of how knowledge was transmitted from one large group of people to another, and how stories, traditions, and mythology was passed on from one generation to the next. You can see a timeline of this in Matt Peters's article "The History of Storytelling in 10 Minutes" (*https://oreil.ly/4amoQ*).

The arrival of data storytelling allows us to put a human perspective on a data set and convey emotion and intuition seamlessly. Data storytelling combines three critical components, storytelling, data science, and visualizations, to create not just a colorful chart or graph, but a work of art that carries forth a narrative complete with a beginning, middle, and end.

Good data stories have three key components: data, narrative, and visuals. You can see a diagram illustrating this from Brent Dykes in Figure 2-6.

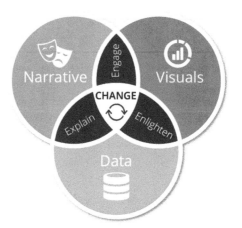

Figure 2-6. The components of an effective data story[9]

The data part is fairly obvious—data has to be accurate for the correct insights to be achieved. The narrative has to give a voice to the data in simple language, turning each data point into a character in the story with its own tale to tell. The visuals are what we are most concerned about. They have to allow us to be able to find trends and patterns in our datasets and do so easily and specifically. The last thing we want is for the most important points to be buried in rows and columns.

As stated by the well-known data visualization expert, Stephen Few, "Numbers have an important story to tell. They rely on you to give them a clear and convincing voice."[10] Therefore if you have an insight that you want to share, it's best to share it in the form of a data story.

Types of Data Visualizations

There are different methods to represent data. Let's discuss some of the most well-known uses for data visualization.

---

9 Image credit: Brent Dykes, *Effective Data Storytelling: How to Drive Change with Data, Narrative, and Visuals*, Wiley, 2020.

10 Jim Stikeleather, "How to Tell a Story with Data," *Harvard Business Review*, April 24, 2013, *https://oreil.ly/WBDwm*.

CHANGES OVER TIME

This is probably the simplest method to teach and to learn, yet no less valuable because of it. Children can plot points based on how many candy bars they sold at the school store over the course of a week to determine what days they should stock the most and what days they can reorder without loss of revenue. They see that more kids are buying candy on Tuesday and Friday—Tuesday because they all remember about the candy on Monday but don't have money until they go home that night to ask for some, and Friday because it's the class snack day and a fun way to welcome in the weekend.

Businesses can chart the popularity of certain items over the course of a quarter, a year, or a decade to see what historical events are influencing their sales and how to prepare for them in the future.

A hotel chain can plot its drop in revenue during years when gas prices soared, such as in 2008 when tensions in the Middle East and the United States' faltering relationship with Argentina drove the price of unleaded gas domestically toward $4/gallon. With fewer Americans taking long road trips and the price of jet fuel skyrocketing, predicating that airlines raise their prices and cut down on the flexibility of how much luggage each person could bring accordingly, far fewer Americans traveled that summer and hotel reservations took a nosedive.

While these numbers impact some when they simply hear them, they garner a much more severe, immediate reaction when they can be seen on a bar chart as a series of tall, vibrant colored lines for each year preceding 2008, then a huge dropoff in number of reservations and corresponding number of dollars earned for 2008. The bounceback that follows only mitigates the damage done, but does not solve the problem should it happen again.

Seeing that visualization (Figure 2-7) helps get people into a problem-solving mode: at what price point in gasoline costs does our revenue start to fall beneath a sustainable level? What are the indicators that this will repeat itself in the future? Since we cannot control the price of gas, what other avenues can we take to combat the drop in revenue when another gas spike occurs?

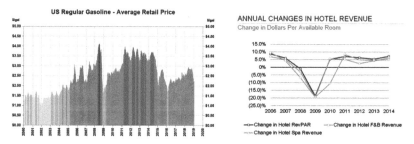

Figure 2-7. Average gasoline prices over the past 20 years (upper graph) and the annual changes in hotel revenue (lower graph)[11]

DETERMINING FREQUENCY

Determining frequency is another basic use of understanding data through visualization that is still powerful and relatable today, particularly if it is coupled with time. If you have ever taken your car to a car wash business, you have likely been asked if you want to join their exclusive membership club where for a flat rate a month, you can get your car washed an unlimited amount of times. Most people say no, but some jump at the opportunity, always eager for a deal if they see it as such. Now turn that scenario around to a data analyst at a car wash chain realizing that most customers bring their cars to be washed on a pretty erratic schedule—most no more than one time a month, and some a lot less than that—typically when there is a coupon online or in the mail, or when they are about to go on a trip out of town or have just returned from one and feel the need for a clean car.

The data analysis shows that there is a small percentage of customers who come a few times a month, and when they do, they tend to spend more money inside the car wash on drinks or snacks or air freshener or various knick-knacks sold, such as bumper stickers, key chains, etc. The ideal then would be to create a program that encourages more visits per month for more customers because the data reads that when people come more often, they spend more money.

By putting this information into a visualization package, analysts can show their executives that by offering an "unlimited wash" program for a flat fee, they will entice more customers to enroll in it because of the free/reduced rate aspects and have the chance to bring in more revenue based on the extra spending.

---

11 Image credits: Robert Allison, "Let's Track the Falling Gas Prices!" SAS (blog), January 15, 2019, *https://oreil.ly/efz2u*; Robert Mandelbaum and Andrea Foster, "Hotel Spa Departments Following Industry Trends," Hotel Online, February 17, 2016, *https://oreil.ly/JyCzl*.

Since very few people come to the car wash two or three times a month, the business will be losing next to nothing in terms of "free" car washes because those who do join the program will be carrying the mentality that since the car wash is free, they can spend a few dollars on extra items while there. Getting a financially minded executive to agree to a program for as many free car washes as you want in a month gets a lot more palatable with the data points when extra revenue comes into play. Figure 2-8 provides an example of this data.

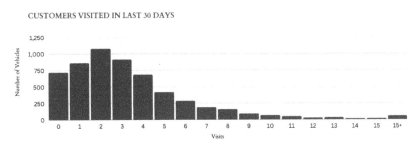

Figure 2-8. Bar chart illustrating the number of vehicles that visited the car wash in the last 30 days[12]

DETERMINING RELATIONSHIPS

The practice of finding relationships between different sets of data—also known as correlations—is the bread and butter of what data analysis, and by proxy data visualization, is all about.

The easiest correlations are simple even without visualization: when the temperature increases in the summer, the average electricity bill goes way up and so do ice cream sales. But others are so subtle that it takes the likes of machine learning to discover them and visualization to make them palatable to human comprehension. Understanding the fundamentals of correlation is the first step forward to making sense of it enough to harness change for the better in a business. Without one, the other cannot go forward. You can see in Figure 2-9 an example scatter plot of temperature versus ice cream sales.

12 Image credit: "Unlimited Car Wash Membership Program," Washify, *https://oreil.ly/Djm4G.*

Ice Cream Sales

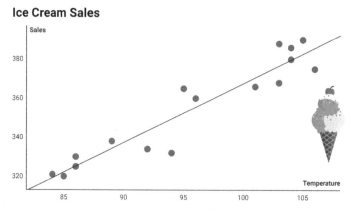

Figure 2-9. Scatter plot showing the rise in ice cream sales as the temperature increases[13]

EXAMINING NETWORKS AND MARKETING

The advance of data analysis in general and data visualization in particular has taken the field of marketing from a nebulous study of impressions and tenuously gathered results to a fantastically structured and highly relatable science of quantifiable metrics that have allowed marketing sales to blend into one superorganism in many industries. Examining a network of customers and how they want to be informed and sold to as well as what message types they respond to is essential for branding, sales, customer retention, and long-term successful relationships.

The advent of being able to collect customer data from sign-up sheets for things like special offers, newsletters, coupons, etc., has opened up a huge window for data analysis. Couple this with gathering data from social media and marketing departments have gone from starving to stuffed in terms of how much information they suddenly have available for processing. But like the other points made earlier, this information is only as powerful as a department's ability to translate it into actionable visuals that tell the tale of what they are seeing.

Convincing the executive powers that your customer base no longer wants to drink champagne toasts at fancy dinner parties but instead wants you to include hot chocolate in your catering service is a tough sell without the data to back it

13 Image credit: Lenke Harmath, "A Focus on Visualizations: Scatter Plot," Sweetspot (blog), May 30, 2014, https://oreil.ly/NCOvC.

up, and unless that data is put together in exceptionally powerful visuals that leave no room for error, you're going to be fighting a serious uphill battle.

Figure 2-10 demonstrates a strong preference for hot chocolate (from our fictitious survey) so you might have a chance at convincing the executives.

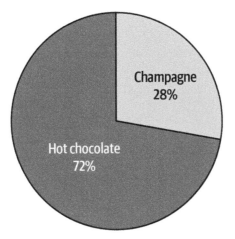

Figure 2-10. Pie chart showing the beverage preferences of hot chocolate versus champagne

You'll notice that for the pie chart in Figure 2-10, we leveraged "natural colors" for hot chocolate and champagne. We selected colors that are associated with the items represented—brown for hot chocolate and a yellowish color for champagne. This makes it easier for our audience to distinguish between the two slices.

SCHEDULING

Has there ever been a happier group of people than schedule makers when understanding data through visualization became available to the general masses in the business world? If you worked in business before the age of the internet, schedule making was one of the most rigorous, mistake-prone, and unforgiving tasks that a company could ask for. But using data based on workers' availability, project due dates, availability of resources and materials, and the power of AI to sort through it all makes things so much easier now.

Even better is the ability of data visualization to structure it all in a way that is easy for anyone to comprehend; the reduction in loss of labor-hours based on being able to easily visualize schedule making is enormous. Figure 2-11 is a great example of a schedule visualized to demonstrate the time spent before and after having a baby.

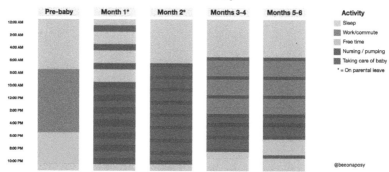

Figure 2-11. Schedule chart showing the allocation of time before and after having a baby[14]

Chart Selector Guide

Hopefully the examples were helpful in getting you familiar with the different ways that data visualization can be used across various industries. Figure 2-12 is a Chart Selector Guide (*https://oreil.ly/7CPhR*) that provides more examples of the different types of data visualizations, as well as sample charts for each category.

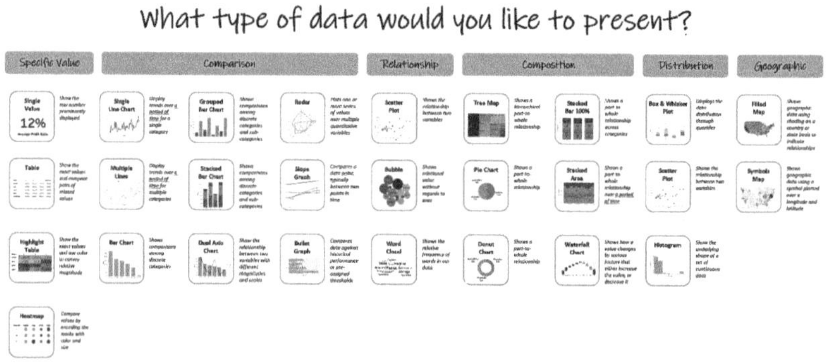

Figure 2-12. Chart Selector Guide

Image credit: Caitlin Hudon, "Schedule Change with a Baby," FlowingData, January 13, 2020, *https://oreil.ly/n8NEq*.

Summary

In this chapter, the main takeaway is that data visualization and data storytelling play a key role in communicating information with stakeholders. We covered the various types of visualizations that can be used when crafting stories with data.

3

Types of Colors Used in Data Visualization

When it comes to data visualization and data storytelling, the types of colors you use are going to make or break your presentation—it's really just that simple. Colors direct our eye movements and thus command our attention and our brain power. Your color usage can either help or hinder the understanding your intended audience gets from the data you are presenting.

Three Types of Colors

There are three types of colors to understand and utilize in your data visualization process. The type of color palette that you use will depend on several things, including the nature of the data you are preparing to bring to life visually. The three types of colors we will be looking at are sequential, diverging, categorical.

Figure 3-1 provides a glimpse into the various types of colors.

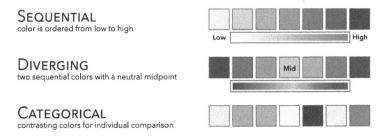

SEQUENTIAL
color is ordered from low to high

Low · High

DIVERGING
two sequential colors with a neutral midpoint

Mid

CATEGORICAL
contrasting colors for individual comparison

Figure 3-1. Demonstration of three types of colors: sequential, diverging, and categorical[1]

---

1 Image credit: Steve Wexler, Jeffrey Shaffer, and Andy Cotgreave, *The Big Book of Dashboards: Visualizing Your Data Using Real-World Business Scenarios*, Wiley, 2017.

Let's break down these three color types and see what circumstances make the most sense for each.

SEQUENTIAL

Sequential colors have numeric meaning and move from light to dark using a graduation of colors. These ordered values use colors assigned to data values, often based on hue, lightness, or a combination of the two.

Typically, the lower values are associated with lighter colors and the higher values with darker colors. However, this depends on the type of background the chart is depicted on. On a white or light background, the lower values are the lighter colors. On a darker background, the reverse is often true. While it works to have a single hue for a sequential color palette, spanning the distance between two colors can also have its benefits and make for a visually stimulating experience. Assuming a white or light background, you can start with a warmer color such as red, yellow, or orange, and trend toward a cooler color (green, blue, or purple) on the darker end of things to give a distinct pattern between the two.

Let's look at an example of how sequential colors can be used for displaying total sales by state using a green sequential color scheme to show the lower sales (light green) and higher sales (darker green) within each state (Figure 3-2).

Monthly Sales by State

Figure 3-2. Map view of sales: demonstration of sequential color usage

DIVERGING

When the numeric variables have a meaningful, central value, such as zero, a diverging palette can be used. It combines two sequential palettes with a shared endpoint that rests on the central value. Those values to the right of center are assigned colors on one side and are typically larger, and the smaller ones sit left of center.

There are usually distinctive hues on each side of center to stagger and separate the positive from the negative values. The central value should have a typically light color so that darker colors can indicate more and more of a larger distance from the center of the range. Such colors to use in this format are red-yellow-blue, red-blue, and orange-yellow-blue.

No matter what kind of colors you are using, the first and most important rule should be to keep it simple. Just like too many witches spoil the brew, too many colors will dilute the meaning and make things confusing for your intended audience. You have to remember that your audience—whether they are potential customers, potential investors, the company's board of directors, or people on the street—are all going into this visualization without much context.

Even if they have read the agenda and presumably know what's coming, they still should be able to take that first 10- to 15-second glance and know what the subject is, what the data represents, and what the story is without having to raise their hands, ask questions, and talk to each other about who sees what. If you pick your colors properly, you're likely to record a slam dunk in this capacity. If you've gone too far off target or you're loading up the entire rainbow into your infographic, an airball is a lot more likely to be in your future.

As an example for diverging colors, observe Figure 3-3, where we display the profitability for each state, with the deep orange colors displaying low profitability and deep blue representing high profitability.

No matter what type of presentation you are making, the use of color plays a vital role in capturing the user's attention and creating specific emotional reactions. Colors can reduce the cognitive load that a person has to commit to understanding the information presented by putting it in a simpler format that emphasizes colors, shapes, and patterns, which are much easier to understand for most people than a complex series of numbers.

Profitability by State

Figure 3-3. Map view of profitability: demonstration of diverging color usage

CATEGORICAL

Categorical colors, sometimes referred to as "qualitative," help their users map nonnumeric meanings for objects in a visualization. They are designed to be easily and visually distinctive from one another. They are optimized so that readers with color vision deficiencies can still read them with minimum difficulty. Typical examples are nominal variables in charts like zip code, blood type, and race.

Emphasizing patterns is the name of the game here, and using darker actionable colors will draw attention to those findings. The colors assigned to each group need to be very distinctive, and as a rule of thumb, the maximum palette size should be seven colors or fewer. Once you get past that number of colors, you can really start having a tough time distinguishing between different groups. If there are more possible values than colors, you should try to bundle some of the values together to make it easier on yourself and not get into a situation where there are such slight differences between colors that it would take the most high-tech monitor in the world to be able to accurately portray the differences. You can also explore breaking the visual into multiple graphs.

For example, if you were breaking down sales for your company by location, and you had sales in 40+ different states, you couldn't possibly conjure up over 40 different distinctive colors (Figure 3-4) to successfully chart out everything.

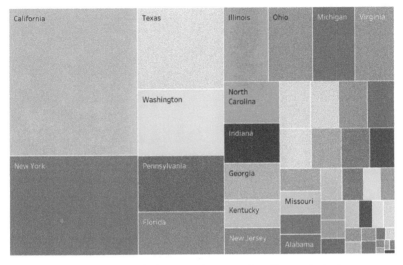

Figure 3-4. Treemap of sales values by location: demonstration of categorical color usage

Instead, you could break down the sales by region—say North, East, Central, and South—and use four distinctive colors from all over the color wheel to really differentiate the values for the reader (Figure 3-5).

The best way to generate distinctive colors is through their hues, specifically by adjusting the saturation and lightness to make them crisp and make them "pop." There should not be any colors that have big differences or where additional lightness or saturation are used because the difference might suggest that some colors are more important than others, unless that is your intention. Additionally, don't use two colors that share the same hue but have different lightness and/or saturation readings on them unless those values are related, as this can cause a lot of confusion.

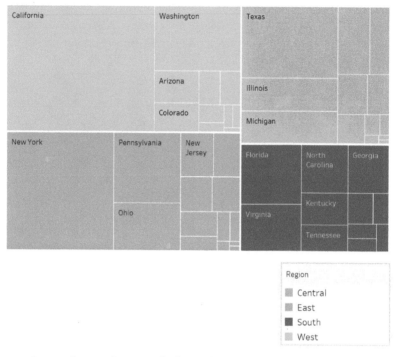

Figure 3-5. Improved usage of categorical colors to demonstrate sales by location

Let's become more familiar with some of these terms. *Saturation* represents how pure the color is—for example, a vibrant orange versus a duller brown with more gray. Colors with high saturation look brighter and more vivid. *Lightness* reflects the intensity of the light in the color—for example, light and dark blue. It's also important for us to define *luminance*, which describes the the perceived brightness of a color.[2]

Background Colors

The background isn't something we think about a lot in most of our creative compositions because, well, it's in the background. A friend of mine has a great photo framed on his desk of himself and four friends from right after their college graduation ceremony, arms linked and big smiles on their faces as they head

---

2 Tyler Wu and Lucy Cui, "Choosing the Right Color Scale for Data Visualization," Psychology in Action, May 19, 2022, *https://oreil.ly/AWQH8*.

out into the future. In the background, there's a woman who has dropped her camera a split-second before and is doing the most awkward lunge/knee bend of all time in an attempt to catch it before it shatters on the ground. Once you've seen her hilarious antics in the back of the photo, it's impossible to see anything else. People tend to get itchy in their data visualization when they're putting out figure after figure that are all produced with white backgrounds. They start worrying that it's coming across as too dull, too stark, too stale. That sort of mental condition is similar to writers and journalists who fear that audiences will get bored when every quote or piece of dialogue ends with the word *said*.

Only through analytics and research do we find that this is usually only a worry of the creator. In a captivating book, the word "said" is barely noticed by the human mind; it's just a placeholder to make us understand that this is dialogue we are reading, not the author's words, but some real person or fictional character.

Likewise, a predominant amount of the time, the person looking at your data visualization piece has not just looked at 50 others and is bored by the white background; they have a specific purpose in seeing the data you've compiled and represented with numbers, colors, etc. That white background is very unlikely to cause them any level of distress.

Note

Remember that the perceived color of an object is not just dependent on the color of the object itself, but also on its background. Different objects grouped by the same color should have the same background. That means that generally speaking, variations in background colors should be minimized.

I love sharing the example of the gray squares (Figure 3-6). There are two squares here of the exact same color; however, because they are placed on a diverging background, you perceive the two squares to be different shades.

Figure 3-6. Two same-colored squares placed on a gray-white diverging background

Our smartphones are a great example of why standard, "boring" white is so well accepted in data visualization. You can turn your phone's background to any color you want, but how many times do you see someone typing away on a phone with a bright red or forest green background? The answer is that you don't because the background is supposed to support what is in front of it, not steal the show. Some folks flip their background to a darker color for night-time use, as those bright screens can wreak havoc in your brain when it's time to wind down and head to sleep. But even that flip job can be distracting because your eye is drawn to what is new and what stands out, and a dramatic change in background color can accidentally cause that to happen.

With so many companies now creating dashboards as part of their offerings, you are seeing more and more colors being used in bad backgrounds that distract from the important information. If you don't use white, a cool gray is a good second choice that doesn't distract from any color and can actually sharpen several of them so that they really stand out.

One of the biggest mistakes people make is using a dark background or a highly saturated color for their resumes. It's not hard to understand why it happens so often; people are looking for any advantage to make their work stand out, to make it "pop." If you've ever been a hiring manager and come across a resume that is printed on bright red paper (back in the days when we had resumes on paper), you know that this is the mark of someone wanting to stand out in the crowd by being what they perceive as unique, but often it is just really, really distracting instead.

Simply put, the reason it's called the background is because it's behind what's really important. The beautiful Hawaiian beach is an amazing piece of scenery, but the newlywed couple smiling in front of it is what all their friends want to see when they post pictures to Facebook from their honeymoon. The grandparents think it is great that you're getting your photo taken in front of Cinderella's Castle at Disney World, but the grandkids' smiling faces in the front are what they're really opening the email for.

Darker backgrounds don't necessarily look bad all the time, but they are still not serving their intended purpose. For starters, a heavy background draws attention away from the data visualization itself, which is the exact opposite of the intended effect.

See Figure 3-7 for an example of how a color-rich background can confuse the audience and how a white background can help the main components of a data visualization stand out.

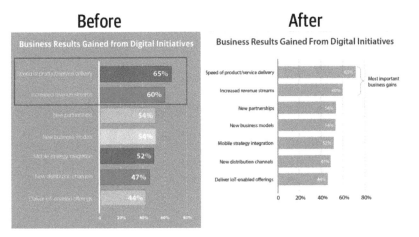

Figure 3-7. Two bar charts: one showing how a color-rich background makes it difficult for readers, and another showing how a white background is more effective[3]

Notice the drastic changes in the visual once the color is reduced to only blue, the weight of the graph lines is slimmed down, and the background is updated to the color white.

---

3 Image credit: Courtney Jordan, "Make Your Data Speak for Itself! Less Is More (And People Don't Read)," *Towards Data Science*, July 7, 2017, *https://oreil.ly/yyZaV*.

We only have one brain and one set of eyes. When they are drinking in the wrong information, they're not getting the value of the data you've trying to put in front of them.

This reminds me of an experiment that a local government office once tried that didn't have the intended results. A local county courthouse was trying to get people entering the building to focus on its new security rules—namely no firearms, no food or drink, and no children allowed in the building. The rules were all posted on a digital sign, but next to the sign was a curious site, a "holographic" police officer who was so life-like that most people did a double-take or a triple-take before they figured out that he wasn't real and that he was just a really cool piece of technology. People would walk up and gawk at the hologram that was mounted on a video board in the exact same shape and size as a regular person, poke and prod it, take photos and videos on their smartphones, and talk to other people in line. Of course, what they did not do is read any of the rules on the sign next to the officer; in fact, most of them were hardly aware the sign even existed! By accidentally shifting the focus, they diminished the message they wanted to send, which is what a really strong, bright, bold background can do as well.

A less well-known but just as legitimate reason to stay away from background colors other than white is that they are distracting and it takes the human brain longer to process it. Black (or other color) words on a white background is our default setting. Switching it up to try and read white text on a black background can be almost as difficult to do for most people as reading the text upside down!

Take a look for yourself at the difference in how quickly you process information.

The lazy sleeping dog was quickly jumped over by the brown, quick fox.

Quick, right? Now, slightly different wording and reversing the basic colors (Figure 3-8).

The lazy sleeping dog was quickly jumped over by the brown, quick fox.

Figure 3-8. White-colored text placed on a black background

It's nothing you would notice in a short phrase or two, but your mind will keep focusing on that black box and trying to make rhyme or reason of why it's there at all instead of noticing the words inside of it.

The Power of Dividers in a Data Visualization

Sometimes, adding a divider to a visualization can help transform it from something that's difficult to understand into a more effective visual.

For example, if we take a look at these two pie charts, you'll notice that by adding a white divider in between the slices of the pie, we can help make each slice a bit more distinct (Figure 3-9).

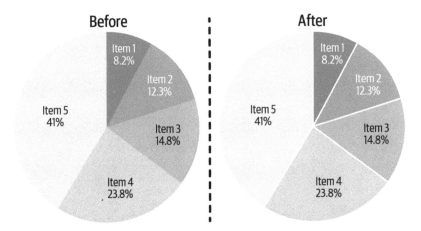

Figure 3-9. Two pie charts demonstrating how a white divider can separate the slices and create a more visually appealing image

Additionally, you can improve the look of other charts, such as treemaps (Figure 3-10) and geographic maps.

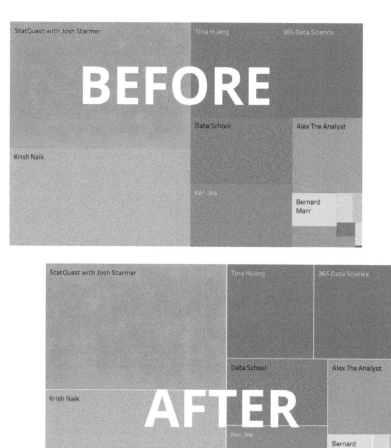

Figure 3-10. Two treemaps demonstrating how a white divider can separate the rectangles and create a more visually appealing image

In the geographic map example, you'll notice that we used black-colored dividers to help make the distinction between each state (Figure 3-11).

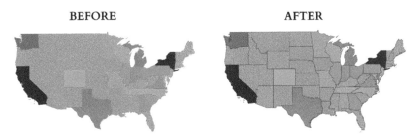

Figure 3-11. Two map views demonstrating how a black divider can separate geographic locations and create a more visually appealing image

Summary

In this chapter we discussed the various types of colors that can be used for data visualization. It's important to understand when to utilize sequential, diverging, and categorical color schemes when designing visuals. Additionally, the proper selection of background colors can either make or break your data visualization. When in doubt of which background color to choose, go with the simple white that is commonly accepted and easily interpreted.

4

How to Tell a Story with Color

It's not enough to merely slap data on a piece of paper or a screen these days; it needs to capture the intended audience's attention, guide them through the story you want to tell, and bring them to the intended conclusion. Here are some quick tips on how to tell a data story with color, which we will expand upon in later chapters.

Keep It Simple

First and foremost, too much of a good thing, even a great thing, can be overwhelming. Data scientist Edward Tufte coined the phrase "data-ink" ratio to describe the amount of ink necessary to put into your data visualization project, and makes the point that excessive amounts of color for the sake of decorative purposes is going to do nothing but be distracting.[1] The right amount of ink gets your points across quickly and easily, and moves the reader through the data as easily as they would if they were reading words on a page in a gripping story. The wrong amount of color confuses the person trying to analyze the infographic and can even hide—accidentally—what they are trying to say.

Too many colors and fancy designs might impress your friends and your school-age children, but they are unlikely to do the same for business associates and consumers. You're not trying to design *USA Today*'s weather map here; you're trying to deliver a specific narrative that can either stand alone or that augments text, video, etc.

---

1 "Edward Tufte," Wikipedia, *https://oreil.ly/sYHbp*.

Charts can make it even worse, because there are even more options, including making things three dimensional for no good reason, using legends to explain complex selections, and toggling text into different colors for no reason whatsoever. Just take a look at the example in Figure 4-1, where we have a 3D bar plot. This chart has several drawbacks, such as being more difficult to find the exact percentages of a bar, green bars are hidden, and for an equivalent value, the green bars in the back appear smaller than blue bars in the front. The chart on the right is easier to interpret after we've removed the 3D effect.

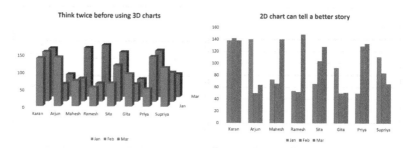

Figure 4-1. Bar chart demonstrating the drawbacks of 3D charts[2]

Now that we've covered some of the pitfalls of using 3D charts, we can see that simple is usually better. Another way to keep things simple is to be intentional about how we treat color legends. Let's briefly discuss how we can incorporate color legends within a data visualization, to make it easier for our audience. Figure 4-2 shows an example of how we can replace the default settings of a color legend that sits off to the side with and alternative chart that doesn't require the reader to keep looking back and forth. The "after" image on the right includes the color legend inside of the chart—with the names of the ship modes (standard, same day, etc.) written directly near the end point of the lines, keeping the text color the same as the line color for further simplification.

2 Image credit: Yan Holtz, "The Issue with 3D in Data Visualization," From Data to Viz, last accessed November 7, 2022, https://oreil.ly/TeGl6.

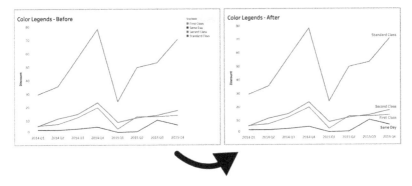

Figure 4-2. Two line graphs: left shows the color legend off to the side and right shows the color legend embedded in the chart

Less ink allows you to gain your audience's attention easier and guide them to the specific points that are most important. Just like when you write content, you put the most important points first because that's what you want the reader to focus on. When you have a data visualization, the color acts as the lead magnet—it draws the audience to the most important point of the data; everything else is secondary and should be treated as such.

Data Story Components

Storytelling in any form combines at least three elements:

- Characters
- Plot
- Narrative

For comparison in a data story, you can switch these up to visual representations. The *characters* are the fields of data to be analyzed, the *plot* is the insight that comes from that analysis, and the *narrative* is the style you are using to communicate that insight to the audience. As creators of visual data representation, we have the most control over the narrative—the way we are able to communicate our insights to draw the user in, get our point across, and do so in a trustworthy way that builds credibility.

That's another danger of the overuse of color. When something starts looking like a cartoon, it's hard to take it seriously. Color is an easy way to control the style that your data visualization embodies. Good use of color makes insights jump off the page, adds professionalism to your brand, and engages the visuals, even if they are dense, complex topics.

Reduce Color Saturation

One tip to keep an audience focused on your story without overwhelming them is to reduce the saturation of the colors, something we spoke about in Chapter 3. In certain cases, when colors are overly intense, they can take away from the message you are trying to send and create confusion in the story you are telling.

In Figure 4-3, we see the difference between using high saturation and low saturation colors when depicting sales figures across product subcategories.

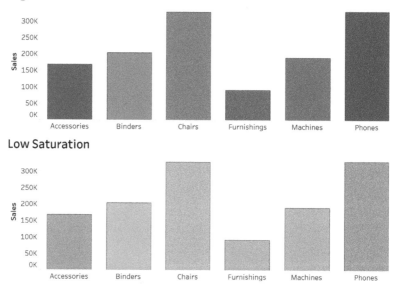

Figure 4-3. Two bar charts illustrating the difference between high and low saturation

As we know from our lessons in primary and secondary colors, and what color psychology is all about, if you have bright yellow or bold red bursting out of a data visualization, it's going to make the presentation all about that color and could easily distract from everything else. Some of the default colors in standard programs are too intense and wind up distracting from the story.

Dulling the hues by reducing their saturation is an easy way to moderate them. You can also change their opacity to about 75–90% to keep the focus on the data with the colors as highlighters. Opacity is the level of transparency of a figure in data visualization. In our example of color saturation, we reduced the opacity by 50% to reduce the level of color saturation.

When you throw a bunch of really bright colors together, you get a story of competition and distraction. That much boldness is not welcome outside of a shirt for the beach or a scoreboard at a professional sports arena. When the colors are slightly muted, you are getting a more mature, professional feel to the story. For an audience, it can be the difference between having information loudly shouted at you and merely shown to you in an authoritative manner.

Color for Highlighting

When you lower the brightness and intensity, you are reducing the cognitive load that your audience has to bear. If you're looking to just highlight one particular piece of data, you can stick with the bright stuff, but place it on just the most relevant piece of data while everything else drops back to grayscale. Figure 4-4 provides an example of using one color to highlight a specific item in a data visualization. In our bar chart, we are highlighting the "binders" subcategory by using an orange color for this bar, and using gray for others.

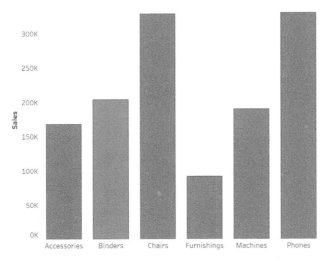

Figure 4-4. Bar chart demonstrating the use of color for focusing your audience on a data point

This allows you to highlight one piece of data and make that the focus of your story without having a myriad of distractions along for the ride.

Color Associations

If you're using more than one color, be very aware of existing associations that come from colors or pairs of colors as they can send your audience spiraling in the wrong direction to the point where they miss the entire point of the visualization.

As we mentioned earlier, red is a very bold, up-front color that is going to instantly draw your attention in most circumstances. Particularly in the United States, red is also a color that warns of danger and negative things. Red lights and stop signs tell you it's time to slam on your breaks, and red marks on a test or a performance review indicate that you didn't do so well, with remedial work likely knocking on your door in the near future (Figure 4-5).

Figure 4-5. Examples of red being used for traffic signals, stop signs, and a failed exam

Similarly, green is usually indicative of positives in society, from its opposition to red in traffic signals to it being the largely accepted color of environmental protection (Figure 4-6).

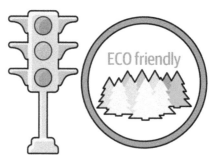

Figure 4-6. Examples of green being used for traffic signals and environmentally friendly signs

Avoid using red and green unless you are very specifically wanting to attach positive and negative connotations to certain things. In a later section, we'll also discuss why you should avoid red and green combinations as it relates to the topic of accessibility.

Try an alternative color pair that matches well together like blue and orange to give a different feel to your story. This is great for simplifying complex stories because the colors pair well together, don't look repetitive, and help the viewer by guiding their eyes. Take a look at Figure 4-7—we are using an orange and blue color combination to show the percent of sales made with first-class and second-class ship modes. The colors are easily distinguishable and do not evoke strong emotions from preexisting associations.

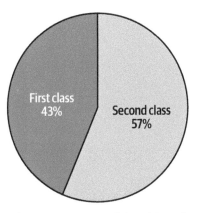

Figure 4-7. Pie chart showing first class versus second class ship modes

You cannot overstate how deeply connected light and color are to emotion.

Power of Gray

When the colors are dull and neutral, they can communicate a sense of uniformity and an aura of calmness. Grays do a great job of mapping out the context of your story so that the more sharp colors highlight what you're trying to explain. The power of gray comes in handy for all of our supporting details such as the axis, gridlines, and nonessential data that is included for comparative purposes.

By using gray as the primary color in a visualization, we automatically draw our viewers' eyes to whatever isn't gray. That way, if we are interested in telling a story about one data point, we can do so quite easily. Take a look at this example where the goal is to highlight the lowest kindergarten vaccination rate for counties in Texas (Terry County) (Figure 4-8).

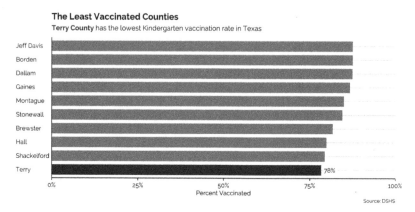

Figure 4-8. Bar chart demonstrating how to use color to focus your audience's attention[3]

This visualization leverages the gray fill of every other bar to immediately draw the audience's eyes to Terry County. Because we used only two colors, we can also highlight text in the subtitle to make the connection even clearer for our audience. Color—if used prudently—makes our visualizations more digestible and more informative.

What do you think would happen if we used a unique bright color for each county? The message would simply get lost amongst all that color (Figure 4-9).

---

3 Image credit: Connor Rothschild, "Color in Data Visualization: Less How, More Why," blog post, June 1, 2020, https://oreil.ly/BHtzB.

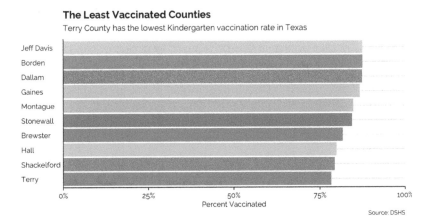

Figure 4-9. Too many colors can confuse your audience[4]

Color Consistencies

Notice that when you want to repeat an idea in a graphic, using the same color can let your audience know that the same thing is being promoted time and again. Take a look at Figure 4-10, where we have a visualization that shows data for Twitter (represented in blue) and data for Facebook (represented in red). If we used a different color for Twitter in the second graph, our audience would get confused.

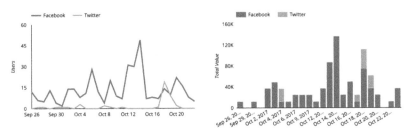

Figure 4-10. Two charts highlighting the importance of using the same color for the same data to ensure consistency[5]

---

4 Image credit: Rothschild, "Color in Data Visualization."

5 Image credit: Benjamin Mangold, "14 Data Visualization Tips You Need to Be Using," Loves Data (blog), October 24, 2017, *https://oreil.ly/6XSIE*.

As a general rule, you should always pick the same color to represent the same thing; be consistent with your color selection and what it represents in your visualizations. Humans naturally perceive color as a pattern, so when they are presented with a color across multiple charts, they will assume it is a representation of the same object or entity.

On the opposite side of things, when the color changes, it lets the audience know that the idea is changing. If you're comparing a pair of business plans, a pair of presidential candidates, or the trials and travels of a pair of sports teams, a change in color is the perfect way to see "Here's Point A, juxtaposed to Point B" without using a single wasted word. Our example in Figure 4-11 demonstrates the use of color change to show when the sales values are increasing or decreasing. We use blue to show increases in value and red to represent decreases in value.

Monthly Sales

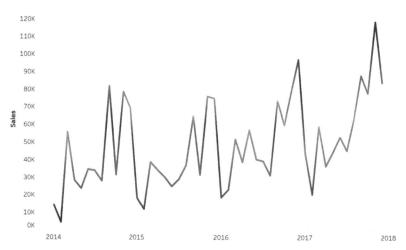

Figure 4-11. Line graph demonstrating the use of color to show when values are increasing or decreasing

Color can carry a story forward without calling attention to itself. It's similar to descriptive words in a novel that is best known for its characters and its dialogue. The reader doesn't understand the impact of the color, but it is a huge part of the overall theme.

Summary

The main point to take away from the chapter is that there are specific tactics used in telling stories with data and this includes specific approaches to using color to deliver insights to your readers. Keep your story simple, pay attention to the color saturation levels, use proper color associations, and keep in mind that the human mind will use color as patterns, so ensure there is consistency of colors across charts that discuss similar items.

5

Selecting a Color Scheme for Your Data Visualization

When people don't take the time to learn about colors, they wind up staggering through project after project with clashing ideas, mismatched pairs, and distracting usage that dooms them before an audience member even tries to discern the meaning of the actual data. Let's take a look at some of the biggest jumping-off points when it comes to selecting a color scheme for your visuals.

Importance of Choosing Colors

Deciding on what colors you're going to use for any project is equal parts exciting and daunting. Exciting because you might stumble across a beautiful combination that takes your data points and creates something truly memorable and unique. Daunting because there's also the possibility that what you create will be a total disaster and convey the wrong message about your brand to the intended audience.

How significant is choosing the right color? Research tells us that more than 50% of people who decide to leave a website and never return do so because of poor color and design choices.[1] No pressure, right? The same holds true for our data visualizations. If you don't capture your audience's attention from the get-go, they're not going to give you the time of day. Just like leaving a website, if

---

1 Neil Patel, "Color Psychology: Meanings & How It Affects You," blog post, last updated May 12, 2021, https://oreil.ly/dbHZj.

your colors don't pop and your message isn't clear, the likelihood of an audience member giving you a second chance is horrifyingly low.

Know Your Audience

A solid first step in picking the best colors for the job is knowing who your target audience is, starting with their culture and country of origin. Different colors mean different things. For instance, in Japan, yellow is a color that represents courage. But in the United States, calling someone yellow typically means they are a coward, and in China, yellow is associated with being vulgar. It's not just culture or country of origin that make a difference when it comes to color, however. Perception is also influenced by gender, religion, social class, race, and age. Doing market research and understanding how your target audience reacts to certain colors and combinations is a vital first step to appealing to them with the data representations that you are concocting. Never start working on a visualization without knowing your target audience front to back, up and down.

Consider Industry Associations

Once you've got your target audience in mind, consider how appropriate certain colors are for certain industries. If you're building a business plot bar graph for the expenditures and revenue of a funeral home, using lime green and hot pink isn't the way to go. Certain colors fit certain industries more than others. Lime green and hot pink might look better highlighting the profit margins of a surf shop in Miami (Figure 5-1).

Figure 5-1. Line graph showing profit changes over time for a surf shop

We don't design a bank's loan reports in bright orange and yellow because we know they don't reflect the seriousness of the industry. We need to be aware of the weight of the things we are preparing. Financial institutions utilize light shades of blue because a majority of people see blue as a color that speaks of trust, honesty, and confidence.

If you're showing off the return on investment for a new dating app, red and pink suddenly become appropriate (Figure 5-2).

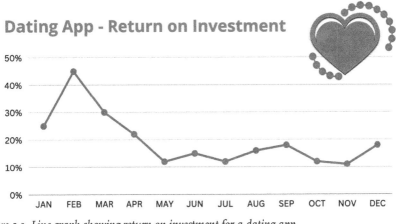

Figure 5-2. Line graph showing return on investment for a dating app

If you are designing a bar graph showing how various companies in the area have reduced their carbon footprints, then the greens and browns of the color wheel that do a good job describing the environment are suddenly in style. Figure 5-3 provides an example of a chart depicting carbon footprints by diet type—you'll notice several greens and browns used in the visual.

Offending the audience with inappropriate colors is a surefire way to lose not only their attention, but also their trust. Don't expect to get either one back once you do.

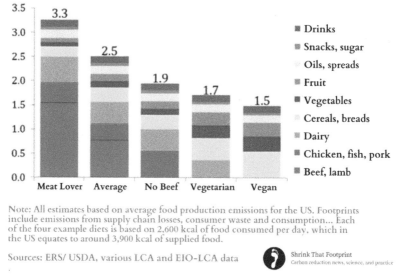

Foodprints by Diet Type: t C02e/person

Note: All estimates based on average food production emissions for the US. Footprints include emissions from supply chain losses, consumer waste and consumption... Each of the four example diets is based on 2,600 kcal of food consumed per day, which in the US equates to around 3,900 kcal of supplied food.

Sources: ERS/ USDA, various LCA and EIO-LCA data

Shrink That Footprint
Carbon reduction news, science, and practice

Figure 5-3. Stacked bar chart showing CO2e per person categorized across diet preferences[2]

Brand Colors

Branding is massively important in the marketing and advertising schemes of your company. If you can get consumers and business partners to identify certain colors with your brand, you're golden (pun intended). When a person sees a certain shade of green and starts wanting a hot cup of coffee (thanks, Starbucks) or sees deep blue and thinks about that great Ford pickup truck their family used to own, the power of color has worked like magic in advertising. But data visualization is not advertising, and the same colors that look lovely on a billboard or an internet ad are not necessarily going to come shining through when you're using them on charts, graphs, and tables.

That mindframe might be counterintuitive and even hard to accept for people in the C-suite who want everything to conform, but your allegiance should not be acting overly agreeable but doing your absolute best to get the data you're in charge of to pop to the audience and represent itself as good as possible. At

2 Image credit: Jane Richards, "Food's Carbon Footprint," Green Eatz (blog), last updated October 14, 2020, *https://oreil.ly/jVCwl*.

any company, a dozen people have probably had their say in brand colors and gone through multiple permutations to get them just right. That usually results in a style guide of some sort that is the unofficial bible of how all company documents and representations must be done to keep that cohesive feeling going on at all times. But here are three reasons why your brand colors might not work so great when it comes to data visualization:

- They don't have enough contrast between them.
- There aren't enough colors.
- The colors don't work for the data.

The challenge becomes to balance the identity of your brand by creating color palettes for different types of data while maintaining adherence with the tenets of color vision deficiency and contrast so that you're not alienating anyone while branding your data uniquely. For example, let's say you work for a company where a specific blue Pantone color is the guide for all charts produced by the company. In 1963, Pantone (meaning "all colors," combining pan and tone) developed the first color matching system. This system allows graphic designers to see exactly what "blue" would look like on paper and provide the printer with the Pantone number to make sure that they got what they wanted.[3] Thanks to Pantone, we now have color consistency for designers, printers, ink makers, and their clients.

Blue is a nice color for a lot of things, but it's tough for people to tell the difference between shades of blue in a report. Light blue and dark blue and royal blue and navy blue have a tendency to run together, so differing shades are not going to make that big of a difference for audience members trying to unspool what's being presented. The same goes for other colors: it's not that easy for humans to tell the difference between varying shades of the same color (unless they are drastic). To showcase data complexity, more colors are going to be needed. You might run into a situation where your superiors aren't going to want to branch outside of your brand colors, so you'll have to make an example of what it will look like to show them why it's absolutely necessary. Don't do it out of spite or malice; just create two versions of the same thing: one using only the approved colors and one using a bit more that shows the improvement. Let the work sell itself.

---

3 Daniella Alscher, "Color Me Confused: What Is Pantone?," G2, June 12, 2019, *https://oreil.ly/krY8h*.

For the example that follows, let's pretend that Figure 5-4 is our client's company logo—we are working with "Candylicious" that happens to have a bright red logo!

Figure 5-4. Candylicious logo

We are tasked with designing a data visualization that compares the taste of Candylicious candy versus our two competitors, Sweetstuff and Goodcandy. The client wants us to use its logo colors for the charts and graphs we design.

The problem is that our audience is based in the US and our chart gets misinterpreted by our audience because when it comes to evaluating performance, Western culture believes that red means bad. In Figure 5-5, you can see a before-and-after chart using the brand colors for a comparison of flavor and variety ratings versus using one color to highlight the company in question—Candylicious—and graying out the rest.

When you're picking those extra colors, don't just randomly grab a few to use and assume that's the only step you need to take, however. You want colors that are going to reflect on your company's brand, and that means doing your homework. Start with the organization's brand guidelines, its mission statement, and any other literature that might exist that talks about what the company stands for, what its touchpoints are, what values it holds dear, and what its motivations to do what it does are.

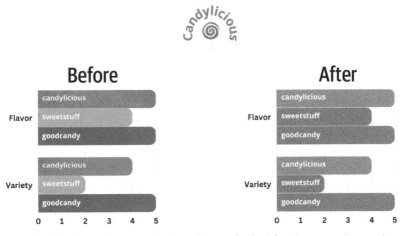

Figure 5-5. Two bar charts demonstrating how the use of red might trigger negative emotions even if they are brand colors

Brand identity is just as important as the brand's colors and can make it a lot easier to pick which complementary colors you want to use in your data visualization. If your company mission statement is big on innovation, toss in some orange. If you're selling trust and historic reputation, consider blue. Don't just settle for the standard colors, though; work on tints and shades that pair up well with your brand colors. You also need to consider contrast between your colors and between the ones you use and the background so that anyone can read and distinguish them. Contrast goes beyond crisp colors, however; it also is vital for people who are visually impaired or have low vision.

Suggested Color Schemes

There are all sorts of websites and apps that will suggest color schemes for you that pair well and have been used to great success in the past. I would definitely suggest a hands-on approach when you're doing your data visualization work—specifically building the graphics, charts, and illustrations in "grayscale mode" first and then applying various colors to them to find what you like best.

Not everything needs its own color in your creation. This is critical to remember because it keeps you honest and keeps you appreciating the point of color in general. When everything is digital and it's not a single cent more expensive to send out something in color as opposed to grayscale, it can become tough to realize that. For those who are still paying extra to print advertisements on paper in color, the weight of each drop of ink is still a factor and typically makes

these professionals a bit more humble and conservative with how they spread out
their usage.

People tend to get overwhelmed by color choices, especially when they realize that there aren't just 10 or 12 that could be used, but literally thousands. That
64-crayon set you got in your annual school supply package has nothing on what
your professional wheels can deliver. But having that giant selection doesn't
mean you should mix and match without a purpose. Remember our poorly
dressed job interview at the beginning of the book? We don't want to smash our
colors together any more in our data representation than we did in that gaudy
outfit.

When you're linking colors together, we want colors that complement each
other and to use saturation and lightness to work for the purpose that you're
after. Like we've said before, if your purpose is to sell Hawaiian shirts on the
beach in Florida, go crazy with those bright colors. For everyone else, subtleness
is a factor in what you pick. Stay away from colors that bleed into each other and
those that don't have very much variance when you alter the saturation or lightness. If you have orange and you lighten it up 25%, it's still very orange, and if
you pair those two together on a graph, you're not going to get much in the way
of contrast. See the stacked area chart in Figure 5-6 that uses four different
orange colors, each with a varying level of saturation; it's difficult to tell them
apart.

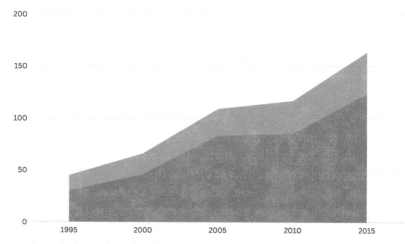

*Figure 5-6. Stacked area chart that shows the difficulty in deciphering between colors closely
related to each other*

A great combination of colors that several data visualization designers like is yellow/orange/red/blue. See Figure 5-7 for an example of a chart that uses these four colors.

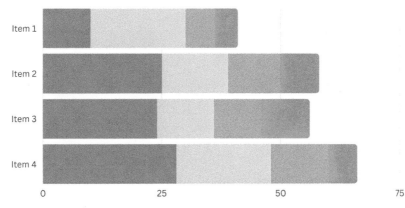

Figure 5-7. Stacked bar chart showing an effective use of color combinations

What's the attraction? You're combining warm colors with cool blue and it makes a difference every time. Even though red and yellow are primary colors that combine to make orange, the three of them are so distinctive that they are easily distinguishable from one another. Plus, blue is the great equalizer for most data presentations. It's so diverse in its shades, and lots of blues can carry the mantle of professionalism, calming, or pleasing emotions whether you use a darker or lighter shade, or full saturation versus just a little bit.

While those four pack a punch, green is surprisingly not as effective in its purest form. See Figure 5-8, which includes green rather than the original blue color in Figure 5-7.

Forest green seems to retract in contrast to other colors, and if you lighten it up, it goes neon pretty quickly, which is an even worse look. But when you lighten it up and desaturate it, you get a very distinct color that holds its value nicely, especially if you add some blue or yellow to it to shift it lighter or darker. Solid green is also a tough sell for people who are colorblind, as it is tough to tell the difference between green, red, and brown.

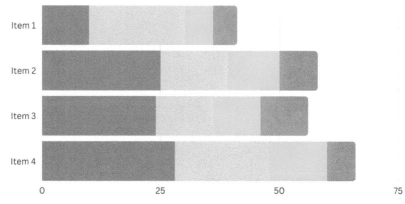

Figure 5-8. Adding green versus blue can make the color combination less effective

Regardless of what combinations you decide on, you need to avoid pure colors that are bright and saturated (Figure 5-9).

Pure colors are primary, secondary, and tertiary colors that haven't had any white, black, or a third color added to them. You can see the pure colors identified on the inner ring of the color wheel above, with the other colors representing tints, tones, and shades of those colors.

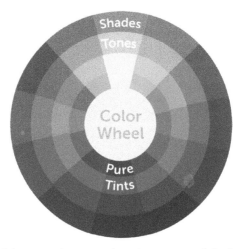

Figure 5-9. Color wheel demonstrating pure colors, tints, tones, and shades[4]

---

4 Image credit: "Color Philosophy #1," Villa30 Studio (blog), March 4, 2018, *https://oreil.ly/L6Mcy*.

Neon colors definitely attract the eye—that's why most of us can't see a yellow highlighter without having a cringe-worthy flashback to studying for a college midterm at 3 a.m. A good example of how frustrating bright neon colors can be is when you put them together in a pie chart or an area chart where they are touching each other without discernible borders. Take a look at Figure 5-10—how is this pie chart making you feel? Overwhelmed?

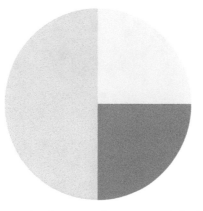

Figure 5-10. Pie chart demonstrating that neon colors are not effective in data visualization

It might seem like a good idea to use those bright colors, but if they all have the same amount of lightness, it's going to be a struggle for your audience to separate them. If you aren't sure if your design fits the bill, convert your colors to black and white. If they are all in the same range of gray, they all have the same lightness and need to be broken up. Let's see the prior neon example in black and white (Figure 5-11)—can you tell the difference between the slices?

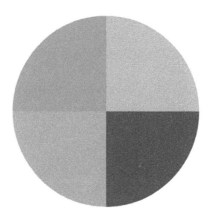

Figure 5-11. How the neon colors appear when printed in black and white

There are two ways to avoid this problem. One is to change the darkness/ lightness of each color to differentiate them; the other is to use a white border to separate one from the other. The first option is usually much better, as the colors will look dynamic and it works better for those who are color blind. Here in Figure 5-12, we have chosen both various lightness for the colors and added the white border to separate the slices.

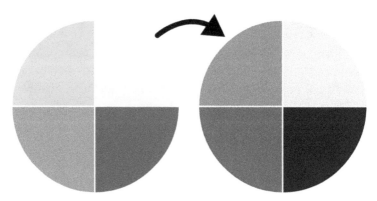

Figure 5-12. Two pie charts that demonstrate the effectiveness of properly selecting colors for each slice (right image illustrates black and white appearance)

Selecting Key Colors in a Palette

So you're going to build a palette for all of your future data visualization needs? You have to start small to get big, and that means selecting a key color that's going to be the standard bearer for everything you do going forward. What is the key color going to represent? It can be a lot of different things, including (but not limited to):

- A color found in an image that compliments the data representation
- The dominant color of your brand
- A color that evokes a certain feel for the data based on predetermined associations, such as blue for financial services institutions or green for an environmental cause
- A color that matches other media in a presentation, such as PowerPoint slides

Regardless of what your reason is, this key color is going to be used in key situations, such as to denote your data points or the point in the presentation that you feel requires the most attention. All of the other colors in your palette will be selected based on how many colors you need overall, where those colors exist on the color wheel, and what sort of relationship the rest of your data has to the key color's data.

For this example, let's say we go with orange as our key color. The orange we go with will have a certain hue, saturation, and lightness associated with it. As we go around the color wheel looking for colors to pair with the key color, we want to keep those hue, saturation, and lightness values the same for each one. This consistency lets us tie the palette together and makes for a very visually pleasing chart, graph, or infographic. Figure 5-13 demonstrates the pairing of orange and blue; we can create a color palette based on the complementary color pairing.

Figure 5-13. Color wheel demonstrating the complementary color pairing of blue and orange

When we change values within the colors, we want to just change one of them—either hue, saturation, or lightness. What we change depends on what we are trying to achieve, but in general if we are using categorical data, we should change the hue to create distinctions. If we are using values or continuous data, we should change the lightness or the saturation.

There are tools available to identify the exact colors used in data visualizations—you can use RGB or HEX values to remain consistent in your content.

RGB is a color spectrum of light using red, green, and blue to render colors on screen. When designing for web, digital, or TV, the RGB color system is used.

HEX, which stands for hexadecimal, is also used on screens and is basically a short code for RGB color. A HEX color is a six-digit combination of letters and numbers. The first two numbers represent red, the middle two represent green, and the last two represent blue. In most programs the HEX number is automatically generated for you.[5]

Figure 5-14 is an example of the RGB and HEX values for the color in the image.

Figure 5-14. Illustration of the HEX and RGB values for a specific color

Using Colors Found in Nature

If you are struggling with selecting a beautiful color palette, you can get inspiration by using colors that can be found in nature. Select a picture that has colors

---

5 Nicole Oquist, "Color Systems Guide - The Difference Between PMS, CMYK, RGB, & HEX," RCP, July 20, 2018, *https://oreil.ly/9v60C*.

you think are beautiful. Here is a nature photo from one of my morning runs around the neighborhood (Figure 5-15).

Figure 5-15. Photo of a river and trees including the key colors in the image

The next step is to pick colors out of them with an eyedropper tool. I use Canva, but you can use Photoshop or other design tools. Take a look at the 18 different colors that were picked out of the nature photo.

You can also use a tool called "Color Thief"[6] to grab the color palette from an image. You can simply drag an image into the browser and identify the key colors used in the image. I dropped in an image (Figure 5-16) from when I took part in a New York City building climb adventure.

---

6 Lokesh Dhakar, "Color Thief," *https://oreil.ly/CzIVB*.

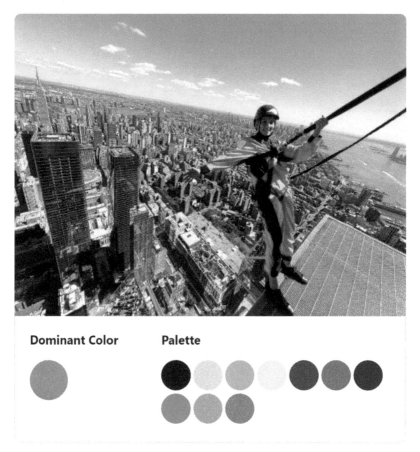

Figure 5-16. Photo of NYC skyline including color palette used in the image

The image provides great views of the city and Color Thief provides us with an effective color palette, along with a suggested dominant color in the image.

Color Palettes for Comparing Two Things

If you're going to compare two things, and the purpose is to make one more important than the other, a smart idea is to use the key color for the one you deem important and use gray for the other one. If you're going to compare two things out of a field of say, a dozen or more, or if there are lots of different elements at play and you want to distinguish a couple of key groups, then you'll likely need to use two different focus colors.

That can be difficult if you don't know your color wheel particularly well. People tend to think about "opposite" colors being necessary or they just pick one bright one and one dark one and roll with it from there. When we are looking for color harmonies for highlighting two series, we can envision a color wheel like the face of a clock with the following colors at the following digits (Figure 5-17):

- 12—Red
- 1—Orange
- 2—Yellow
- 3—Light green
- 4—Green
- 5—Blue-green
- 6—Light blue
- 7—Blue
- 8—Indigo
- 9—Purple
- 10—Pink
- 11—Pinkish-red

Figure 5-17. Color wheel in the form of a clock

Let's run through a few scenarios on how to pick two colors for comparisons in data visualization.

ANALOGOUS HARMONY

Analogous harmony is the easiest to understand and the easiest to achieve. Start with your key color, move exactly one color over to the left or right of it on the color wheel, and use the same level of saturation. Using one or two neighboring colors makes sure that none of them are emphasized more than the others. If your key color happens to be your brand's color, it might make an audience give it a bit of extra scrutiny, but not to the point where it alters their view of the graphic. So for the sake of this example, let's say our selected key color is orange. On the color wheel described in Figure 5-17, one step to the left would be red and one step to the right would be yellow. Both of these are analogous with orange, complementing it well. Figure 5-18 provides a look into the color palette that's created from neighboring colors of orange.

Figure 5-18. Color wheel demonstrating analogous colors

COMPLEMENTARY HARMONY WITH A POSITIVE/NEGATIVE CONNOTATION

While your key color can be well supported by the colors near it on the color wheel, it can be much more strongly supported by the colors on the opposite side. Complementary colors are direct opposites and offer the very best contrast possible. That makes them good for showcasing positive and negative differences.

When you are using your brand's main color as your key color, it works perfectly because it can be the positive in the equation and the complementary color can be the negative. Try to stay away from using your brand color as a negative, even if it is something like red or black, which is often used to mean something negative. To match complementary colors, draw a line from one spot on the color wheel clock face to the number directly across from it. In our orange example, it matches up with blue (Figure 5-19).

Figure 5-19. Color wheel showing complementary colors

Other combinations (Figure 5-20) in this format are:

- Yellow and indigo
- Light green and purple
- Green and pink
- Blue-green and reddish-pink
- Light blue and red

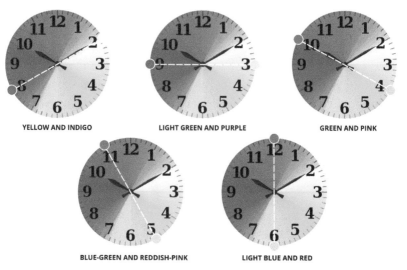

YELLOW AND INDIGO   LIGHT GREEN AND PURPLE   GREEN AND PINK

BLUE-GREEN AND REDDISH-PINK   LIGHT BLUE AND RED

Figure 5-20. Examples of complementary colors on various color wheels

NEAR COMPLEMENTARY HARMONY FOR HIGHLIGHTING TWO SERIES WHERE ONE IS THE PRIMARY FOCUS

Instead of using polar opposite colors, in this motif you can still get good contrast without any possible reason to believe the colors are complementary. This is achieved by going just 33% of the way around the color wheel instead of the full 50%. So if our example of orange is at 1 o'clock on the clock face, its near-complementary color could be found by going 33% forward to 5 o'clock, which is blue-green, or 33% backward to 9 o'clock, which is purple. Ideally in this situation, your key color will be warm and your complementary colors will be cool, but if this is not the case, you can mute the secondary color by decreasing its saturation or altering its lightness so it has less contrast with the background (Figure 5-21).

Figure 5-21. Color wheel with near complementary colors

What are "warm" and "cool" colors? Figure 5-22 demonstrates how the color wheel can be split into warm and cool colors.

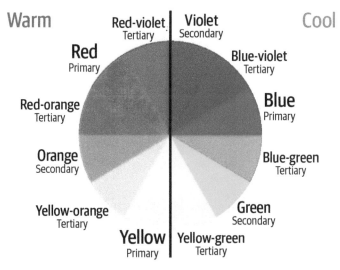

Figure 5-22. Color wheel identifying warm and cool colors

On the color wheel of primary and secondary colors, the warm colors are red, yellow, and orange. Colors that have a red, yellow, and orange hue will also be warm. On the contrary, green, purple, and blue are cool, thus colors that lean towards these tints will be cool too.

Warm and cool colors are categorized as warm and cool due to the feelings that one gets when looking at the hues. Reds, yellows, and oranges make us think of the sun and fire. Therefore, they tend to convey a sense of warmth and comfort. Cool colors, on the other hand, make us think of grass and water. These hues often feel cool and refreshing, much like the outdoor areas that they are associated with.

Color Palettes for Comparing Three Things

Moving from two color palettes to three colors is a bit like taking the training wheels off your bike and suddenly getting on a Harley Davidson. We want to use colors that are visually pleasing to our intended audience, but we also need to imply specific relationships among the different data points that make sense to the audience in an intuitive form. Here are a few examples, based on the same clock face color wheel we used earlier.

ANALOGOUS/TRIADIC HARMONY FOR HIGHLIGHTING THREE SERIES

Analogous harmony works when you are making simple distinctions among categories. This is the simplest of the bunch, as you simply use both neighboring colors to your key color. So for our key color of orange, we would add red from one side and yellow from the other to accent our key color. Because it is familiar from our branding, the key color will have a slightly stronger visual emphasis, but that typically works well for our purposes. Figure 5-23 shows the color palette for comparing three things.

Figure 5-23. Color wheel showing analogous triadic colors

Triadic harmony grabs your key color and the two complementary colors that are evenly spaced around the color wheel. There is more contrast here than with analogous harmony. It will look better on a big screen as a result. The weak point is that you will lose the feeling of one color being the key color.

HIGHLIGHTING ONE SERIES AGAINST TWO RELATED SERIES

In this arrangement, your key color is one side of the wheel and the other two are on the opposite side of it, each one step away from the complementary color we discussed in the previous section. So with orange as our key color and blue as its complementary color, we move one click over to indigo on the left and light blue on the right and add those to the equation (Figure 5-24).

Figure 5-24. Color wheel demonstrating one series versus two related series colors

This is a good formula when you're going to use the two complementary colors as parts of a whole represented by the key color. For instance, if your key color of orange represented the total revenue generated by a school's athletic booster club, indigo might represent donations gathered at the annual golf tournament and light blue could represent sales from T-shirts and other merchandise (Figure 5-25).

Figure 5-25. Treemap demonstrating a color palette for two complementary colors for parts and one representative of the whole

Color Palettes for Comparing Four Things

The need to compare four distinct things with four distinct colors in one visualization is rare. We know from previous experience in this book that we are trying to use color to focus attention, which is considerably difficult with so many colors working at the same time. But it does happen from time to time, and we need to be prepared to handle it when it does.

ANALOGOUS COMPLEMENTARY FOR ONE MAIN SERIES AND ITS THREE COMPONENTS

Analogous harmony is still possible with four colors, assuming you've got the size and contrast to make it work. Take our key color (still orange) and add its complementary color (blue). Now take one step in both directions away from that blue, adding light blue and indigo, and you've got your quartet. The similarities of the three complements allow your key color to easily stand out (Figure 5-26).

Figure 5-26. Color wheel showing analogous complementary colors for one series and three components

DOUBLE COMPLEMENTARY FOR TWO PAIRS WHERE ONE PAIR IS DOMINANT

A likely scenario when there are four different data series is that there are two groups of two series. If that's the case, then double complementary harmony makes sense as the choice to go with. Start with your key color and pick one of its two analogues—the two colors that reside adjacent to it on the color wheel. Now choose the complements of your key color and the analogue to serve as their partners in the pairing. If at all possible, it's very helpful for your key color and its analogue to both be warmer colors and the complementary colors to be cooler colors (Figure 5-27).

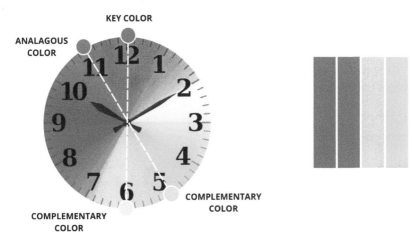

Figure 5-27. Color wheel showing two pairs where one is dominant

RECTANGULAR OR SQUARE COMPLEMENTARY FOR FOUR SERIES OF EQUAL EMPHASIS

If your objective is to use colors to make categorical distinctions across four series where none is more important than the rest, then a square/rectangular harmony can do the trick. Similar to the double complementary, you take the key color and its complementary, but instead of using an analogue, you select a near analogue—two steps away on the clock. Then you take that near analogue's complementary and you've got your rectangular pattern. In square or rectangular harmony, also known as tetradic harmony, you begin with the key color and go every third step around the clock to form your quartet (Figure 5-28).

Figure 5-28. Color wheel showing rectangular harmony

While the rectangular harmony suggests that the four series are really two pairs, the square harmony puts the four colors far enough apart that they all possess equal footing from one another.

Summary

The key point to remember is that you shouldn't accept the default settings within a data visualization software—unless you get lucky and those settings help you tell your data story effectively. Take the time to intentionally select the appropriate color palette that will help you communicate your insights to your target audience.

6

Data Visualization Color Tips

Blending colors together in the form of data visualization is a dance, something subtle, not the equivalent of a new age painter hurtling a gallon of paint on a blank canvas and calling it art. You are looking to influence the overall feel of the creation and give it depth. Think about the definition of the colors you are using. Bright, airy colors like yellow and orange can promote a cheerful sense in someone, bringing happiness, light, and joy into their mood. If you need calm and confidence, blue comes to mind. If you're trying to deliver the excitement of a new product, you can't go wrong with bright red.

Use Contrasting Color

Don't keep using the same color over and over again, regardless of if it's the one most often associated with your brand. If all plotted points are light blue, what's to make one stand out from all the rest? The key here is contrast, as we'll discuss at length a bit later in this chapter.

Contrast between two colors can make a world of difference in the look and significance of your data. If some elements are less important than others, don't waste a color on them; mark them with gray to ensure your important points are accented and everything else does not stand out.

Let's say we are looking at the popularity of specific vegetables in our fictious supermarket. The head of the sales department wants to know specifically how "lettuce" popularity trends look over the past few years (Figure 6-1). We can use gray and green to allow for enough contrast so that the reader can easily distinguish between the trends of various vegetables and the specific one in question—lettuce.

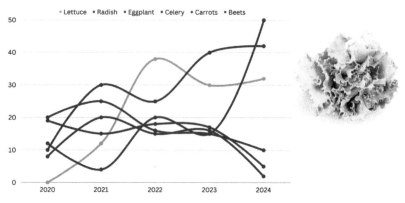

Figure 6-1. Line graph demonstrating popularity of various vegetables, highlighting lettuce

Avoid Bright Backgrounds

A big part of standing out is making sure the audience is focused on the right thing. Having a bright background color might be unique, but it's going to distract the eyes of the person who's looking at your data for guidance. Don't make it hard on them! Look at the two images in Figure 6-2—we have one chart with a bright background and one with a plain white background. Which of these are you able to read and understand more efficiently and effectively?

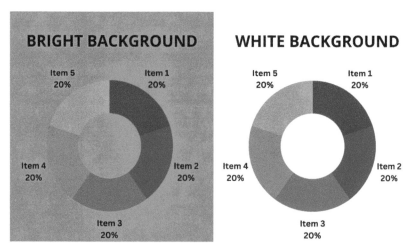

Figure 6-2. Two donut charts illustrating how a white background is superior to a bright background for ease of reading a graph

Know Your Devices

Make sure you know what context your data visualization will be used in. Looking brilliant on the monitor does not mean it will look as glorious on a tablet, phone, or a digital projector that 500 people are going to be staring at. You should also consider the fact that some might end up printing your visualization in black and white!

When discussing color best practices with Maureen Stone, retired research scientist at Tableau, she told me it's important to "get it right in black and white." This is a phrase she has picked from designers and is a fundamental principle in designing with color. As an example, when cartographers design maps, they first design it to be readable in black and white. They will add color at times to make interpretation just a little easier. This is what we must do as data visualization designers: create in black and white and add color to help our readers understand the message more efficiently and effectively.

Use Gradients

If you are having trouble figuring out how to compare and contrast data without having to use too many different colors, consider using a gradient. Use lower gradients on lighter colors and higher gradients on darker colors to show the difference between the two, a comparison that should be intuitive to the audience you are designing for. Figure 6-3 provides an example of how a gradient color scheme can be used to represent the median age across a region. The darker colors are reserved for higher median age and the lighter colors are used for the lower median age.

We should avoid using gradients for categorical data as it will lead to audience confusion.

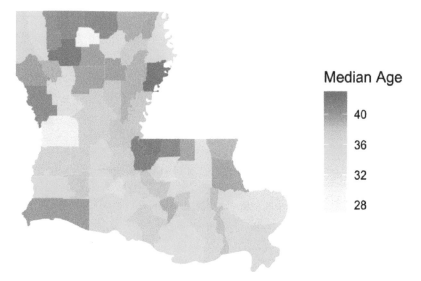

Figure 6-3. Gradient color map view demonstrating median ages, geographically[1]

Summary

In this section, we shared some tips on using color for data visualization and storytelling. It's important to use contrasting colors, avoid bright backgrounds, and design visualizations that can be viewed effectively across various devices (laptop, mobile, print, etc.).

---

1 Image credit: Amanda West, "Pretty (Simple) Geospatial Data Visualization in R," *Towards Data Science,* June 26, 2020, *https://oreil.ly/z52ib.*

7

Accessibility and Addressing Color Blindness

Color vision deficiency, or color blindness, means viewing colors differently than most people, which can often make it very hard to tell the difference between similar saturations of different colors. It's not a problem that gets much play in the media or in the public eye except on rare occasions when it becomes a national issue. In this chapter we'll discuss the importance of selecting colors that are easily interpreted by those with color vision deficiency and cover some best practices on how to address the issue.

Why It Matters

Let's discuss a circumstance when color blindness was highlighted publicly. In November 2015, the National Football League tried an experiment during a football game between the New York Jets and the Buffalo Bills. Normally, the Jets wear green pants with white jerseys or the opposite, and the Bills wear some combination of red, blue, and white depending on if they are playing on the road or in their own home stadium. During the NFL's "Color Rush" campaign to celebrate the 50th anniversary of the league's first-ever TV game shown in color, both teams dressed in solid color pants and jerseys: green for the Jets, and red for the Bills. The result was total chaos for NFL fans who are red/green color blind, who could not tell the teams apart besides the icons on their helmets (Figure 7-1).[1]

---

1 John Breech, "Bills-Jets Game Is Complete Torture for Color-Blind People," CBS Sports, November 12, 2015, *https://oreil.ly/aUksp*.

Figure 7-1. Two football teams wearing green and red uniforms

The website Deadspin took the protest a step forward by using photo-enhancement effects to give an idea to the rest of the world as to what the game looked like through the eyes of a color-blind person. The result? Twenty-two players wearing identical jerseys of muddy green playing on a dingy green field—the bright green turf is also rendered a different shade by color blindness.

We can take the previous image and run it through a color vision deficiency filter to get Figure 7-2.[2] The color vision deficiency filter portrays the most severe case of color-blindness. There are several variations and progression levels of color-blindness, based on individual cases.

---

2 Coblis - Color Blindness Simulator, *https://oreil.ly/bmKtk*.

Figure 7-2. Two football teams with uniforms that look almost identical once viewed in a "color vision deficiency" filter

The embarrassing turn of events happened twice more in 2015, with the all-yellow Rams versus the all-green Seahawks and the all-brown Browns versus the all-purple Ravens. The following season, the NFL admitted its mistakes and altered the campaign to have one team wear all white to help keep the fans out of the dark.

Research shows that about 1 in 12 men (8%) and 1 in 200 women (0.5%) have some form of color impairment, another term for color blindness.[3] Most people can still perceive color, but certain colors are transmitted to their brains with different encoding. Most are not aware that the colors they perceive as identical appear different to other people. Red-green dichromatism is the most common form, where red and green appear indistinguishable. Someone with red-green color vision deficiency would generally be able to distinguish between a bright red and a pale green—though they might not be able to tell which one is red and which is green.

---

3 "About Colour Blindness," Colour Blind Awareness, *https://oreil.ly/JQfh1*.

You have probably come to the conclusion that this is a key point to consider when selecting colors for data visualizations.

Potential Causes of Color Blindness

Many other color impairments also occur in pairs. Very few people are completely color blind, but the ones who are also have trouble with how bright colors are and what different shades they are. Those with severe cases can also have trouble with quick side-to-side movements and sensitivity to light. People are more prone to color blindness if they have a history with the disease, have certain other eye diseases like glaucoma, certain health problems like diabetes, multiple sclerosis, or Alzheimer's, take certain medicines, or are Caucasian.[4]

While you might not know anyone who identifies themselves as color blind, as we mentioned earlier, about 1 in every 12 men and 1 in every 200 women is color blind. That's enough of a frequency to make it something to be aware of if you are doing a data visualization presentation in front of a large audience, or if the dashboards you are using are going to be distributed to a large number of people.

This is just another reason to stay away from the red-green combination in presentations where people where people from Western cultures will tend to associate green with good results and red with negative ones, even if the company in question frequently uses red in its branding.

If you know or work with someone who is color blind, you can have them look over your work before you submit it for approval or for a larger audience. This not only allows you to know what they can see and what they cannot, but also gives you really great feedback on what colors pop for them and which are muddied or muted.

You can also use color vision deficiency filters online by uploading your completed file and viewing it as if you had color blindness. I suggest using the Coblis Color Blindness Simulator (*https://oreil.ly/bmKtk*). You can also check out Color Oracle (*https://colororacle.org*), a free color blindness simulator for Windows, Mac, and Linux. It takes the guesswork out of designing for color blindness by showing you what people with common color vision impairments will see in real time.

Do you want to take a quick test to see if you have color blindness?

---

4 "Color Blindness," National Eye Institute, *https://oreil.ly/8DjVN*.

Try out the quick Ishihara test,[5] which includes circular plates (Figure 7-3) that have printed digits on them that are created by unique random dots in more than one color. Are you able to see all of the numbers in the circles? This will give you a sense for your ability to distinguish between color pairings.

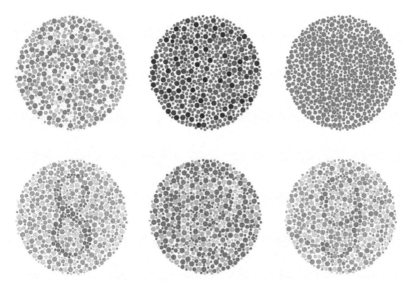

Figure 7-3. Four circular plates that contain multicolored dots that form digits in each circle[6]

The full test can be taken online (*https://oreil.ly/WvgpW*) and includes selecting a number 0 to 9 each time a new circular plate is presented—there are 38 different circles. If a person makes some mistakes during the test, they are diagnosed with color blindness. I took the test and got a result of "normal vision."

Color Combinations to Avoid

Let's review some color combinations that you should avoid if you know there are individuals in your audience that potentially have color blindness.

---

5 "Ishihara Test | Color Test | Ishihara Chart," *https://oreil.ly/WvgpW*.

6 Image credit: "Ishihara Test."

Red, green, and brown

In a field of shades of red, green, and brown, people who are red blind will see nothing but shades of brown, mostly indistinguishable, and a few dark yellows. For people who are green blind, the colors are a little richer, but no green and red exist. People with this color weakness have to wear special glasses or use other aids to drive safely given the preponderance of red and green usage in traffic signals.

Pink, turquoise, and gray

While not exactly the most commonly used group of colors, they do show up often when comparing information in bar graphs and charts. For red-blind people, the entire spectrum looks gray, with the exception of dark pink, which looks more blue. For green-blind people, the light versions of all three colors look muted pink, and the darker ones are a uniform dark gray.

Purple and blue

For both red- and green-blind people, purple just doesn't show up at all, and looks like blue.

Best Practices

If you want to cater to the color blind in your audience, our old friends blue and orange are a great place to start. The old color saying, "Blue is the safest hue" is in full effect here. Orange is blue's complementary color, placed as far away as possible on the color wheel, giving those with color issues the best chance of seeing it clearly.

As I mentioned earlier, a common mantra of design teachers is "Get it right in black and white." Meaning once you've finished your work in color, print it out in black and white. If you can still read it and understand it with a lack of color, then you can have great confidence that someone with color blindness will be able to do likewise.

You can also play with the lightness of the various colors to make them more distinguishable from one another. Adjusting their hue and saturation will not have the same desired result. Another thing to consider is that the more colors you have, the more difficult it is for anyone to tell them apart, especially those who are color blind. In fact, more people notice their own cases of mild color blindness when they look at a presentation with a wide range of colors in it, because they will see two blues, or two other colors that look very similar to them, but different to others.

If you are still struggling with getting a final product that is done right while being sensitive to the needs of the color-blind population, consider other differentiators in your data visualization, such as symbols, shapes, positions, patterns, different line widths, dashed lines, direct labels, and visual effects.

Summary

Keep your audience in mind. If any members of your audience have color blindness, you must take action and intentionally use colors that are easily distinguishable for everyone. The main objective of using colors in a data visualization is to help tell a story, not to confuse your reader.

8

Color and Cultural Design Considerations

As we have talked about in previous chapters, colors carry weight across different cultures with different meanings. That is a tricky thing to realize when working in data visualization, especially if you've lived or worked in one country for a long time and have culture-laden connotations about what each color means.

Colors give specific definitions to different population segments. For instance, in the US, if you see green electrical wires, they are known for grounding a current. If you see a delivery truck driving around with a brown paint job, you know it's a representative of UPS. And if your computer monitor suddenly goes blue, you know it's time to get out the credit card because you've just encountered the Blue Screen of Death and you are in need of a new computer.

Again, be aware of your audience! The world is growing bigger and bigger in terms of population, but our remarkable achievements in technology have shrunk the space between us like never before. Making a business call from New York City to Tokyo a few decades ago would have seemed like an enormous chore. Now it can be done free of charge within seconds via the likes of Skype or Zoom.

Build the portfolio of who you are constructing visualizations for and use that as your base of operations to design something that keeps the focus where you want it. Let's discuss some other examples to build a knowledge base around.

Yellow

In Western cultures like the US, yellow is often seen as the color of warmth and happiness. It is the color of the sun and ties in closely to thoughts of vacations, youth, and fun. However, calling someone yellow implies you think they are a coward. In Germany, it is the color of envy, and in France, it can be seen as being a sign of weakness and betrayal. Across the Pacific Ocean, it is the color of harmony in some parts of China, but vulgar in others. It is the color of luck in Thailand and represents good fortune in Egypt. Yellow is the most visible color on the spectrum and the first one that the eye notices as well. It's also a sacred color in Polynesia, where the word for yellow translates into "food of the gods." Yellow and gold are interchangeable in the Christian religion, and it is thus used to symbolize faith and divine glory. All in all, it's a color that is pretty unlikely to offend anyone in your presentation.

Blue

Although it is often associated with sadness—the very definition of the character Sadness in Pixar's 2015 family hit *Inside Out*—blue has very few negative cultural connotations around the world, which is why it's probably so frequently used by international corporations. For cultures with ties to water—lakes, rivers, and oceans—blue reflects the color of life, survival, calm, and cleansing. It is often seen as having the power to repel evil and offer protection in cultures in the Arab and Mediterranean regions. Because it is such a calming color, many airlines use blue on the inside of their crafts to help calm passengers who might have anxiety about flying. In ancient Egypt, blue was the color of divinity, and in Hinduism, the gods all have blue skin. Occasionally, companies can run afoul of bad connotations, such as Pepsi did in Southeast Asia, when it changed the color of its vending machine to a lighter shade of blue to try and add some distinction. It paid off in quite a different way, as the color was linked to death and mourning in that part of the world!

Red

Red is a striking color with a whole lot of different meanings. In the United States, it means excitement and love, but is also the color of danger and warning signs. Red is also tied to high fashion and glamour in the US—the red carpet rolls out before a big movie premiere in Hollywood, and female movie stars paint their lips red before a night out on the town. In China, red is a symbol of strength and power, most likely tied to the country's Communist history. It has meanings of luck and prosperity as well. In East Asian stock markets, red is used when there is a huge rise in stock prices. When Americans see red on their investment boards, it's usually a sign that it's time to start panic selling. Weddings often use red in China, while in African countries the color has the connotation of death and aggression. In South Africa, it is the color of mourning. Part of that country's flag is painted red to represent the bloodshed and sacrifice that was paid to gain independence, while in Russia, it is historically tied to the Communist ways of leaders like Lenin and Stalin—and thus quite polarizing between those who believe that country's best days are behind it, and others who believe the best days are still to come. Needless to say, red has very strong, often very passionate meanings regardless of what audience you're catering to, meaning you need to be very careful how you use it at all times.

White

Pureness, simplicity, innocence, and weddings all swirl around white in the US. If you don't get married in a white wedding dress, you'll get certain looks on your big day. White is rarely used in data visualization other than as a background, but if you do have a cause to use it, remember that it's not so simple for everyone. For most of Asia, it is linked to death and bad luck. A white feather or a white flag speaks of cowardice and surrender. Japan stands out as a country where white is sacred, but in India, it reflects upon the cycle of death and rebirth. The Pope has worn white since 1566 to symbolize sacrifice, while Muslim pilgrims wear white attire to signify that before God, they are all equal.

Black

Ominous and powerful, black is a lot like white despite being its polar opposite. In India, it is the color of bad luck. A Japanese company marketed its line of successful scooters to India until it realized the meaning of black and had to recall tens of thousands of them to give them all a paint job as no one wanted to buy an unlucky scooter. Black suggests elegance and luxury, but in the US, it is also the color of death. Everyone wears black to a funeral, and the Grim Reaper (allegedly) wears a black robe when he comes looking for you at the end of your life. Black cats are thought to be bad luck in the West, while in Africa, the color symbolizes masculinity, maturity, and age.

Green

There's natural green pretty much everywhere in the world, and for those in the West it's exceptionally popular, representing positive things like being environmentally friendly, having good luck, loving nature, and ,of course, the color of American currency. In Ireland and Mexico, green is the national color, but not everyone holds such a high opinion of it. It's tied to infidelity in China and has a connection with jealousy in many other countries as well—hence the term "green with envy." In Europe, it can also be associated with illness—thus the term "green around the gills." Overall, green is up there with blue and yellow as colors unlikely to do too much long-term offending.

Orange

Our old friend from all those examples earlier in the text, orange has lots of friendly meanings. It is tied to safety in many countries, as it is the color best seen in dim light, and thus painted onto life rafts, life jackets, and safety cones. It is sacred in the Hindu religion of India and represents fertility in Colombia. It is the symbol for love in multiple Eastern countries, as well as health and happiness. In Ukraine, it signifies bravery. In the US, it has come to be linked with innovation in businesses and is often used in the logos of startups, particularly in the tech industry. Of course, nobody's perfect, and even orange has its bad days, like in Egypt where it symbolizes mourning. Meanwhile, in the Netherlands, the phenomenon known as "Oranjegekte" (orange craze) started as a way to celebrate the Dutch royal family—the House of Orange-Nassau—but has since evolved into a way to celebrate the king's birthday along with the country's major sporting events like the F1 Dutch Grand Prix auto race.

Purple

Purple holds the powers of magic, mystery, royalty, and religious faith in both Europe and the United States. It also has symbolism with ambiguity because it is a mixture of red and blue and is used in the bisexual pride flag. In other cultures, purple symbolizes death and mourning. In Thailand, widows wear purple to funerals, and Catholic mourners do the same thing in Brazil. Italians associate purple with funerals, which is why they won't use purple wrapping paper and brides shun the color when planning their weddings. Most Italians even consider it bad luck to wear purple to the opera.

Pink

Pink is widely associated with femininity in the West, and even in many countries in the East. Love, romance, the birth of baby girls, and tenderness also go with it. Pink is thought to be a mentally stimulating color that can reduce violent behavior and help people feel calmer. Although you probably shouldn't mention it in any data visualizations you work on, pink is often used to paint walls inside of prisons to make the inmates more docile. In Japan, both genders wear pink, and it relates more to men than women. In Korea, it means trust, and in Latin America, it has ties to architecture. Interestingly, China ignored the color pink for decades because of its connotations with Western culture. When it eventually entered Chinese culture, the word for it translated to "foreign color."

An interesting fact that my daughter shared with me (she learned this in first grade)—the color pink used to be more popular for boys versus girls in the US. A June 1918 article from the trade publication *Earnshaw's Infants' Department* said, "The generally accepted rule is pink for the boys, and blue for the girls. The reason is that pink, being a more decided and stronger color, is more suitable for the boy, while blue, which is more delicate and dainty, is prettier for the girl. In 1927, *Time* magazine printed a chart showing sex-appropriate colors for girls and boys according to leading US stores. In Boston, Filene's told parents to dress boys in pink. So did Best & Co. in New York City, Halle's in Cleveland, and Marshall Field in Chicago."[1] As we know, this changed over the years and if you walk into a department store baby clothes section, you'll notice the majority of baby girl clothes will be pink, while baby boy clothes will be blue.

Figure 8-1 shows that back in the late 19th century and early 20th century, it was typical for parents to be told that boys should be dressed in a masculine colors like pink to grow into a more manly individual later in life, while girls should be dressed in a more feminine alternative like blue.

---

1 Jeanne Maglaty, "When Did Girls Start Wearing Pink?" *Smithsonian* Magazine, April 7, 2011, *https://oreil.ly/hJLAV*.

Figure 8-1. Photo of a boy and girl wearing dresses, the boy wearing pink, and the girl wearing blue[2]

Summary

The main takeaway here is to avoid misleading with colors at all costs. If you serve up a data visualization, and the audience's first reaction is to be offended or wonder what in the world you were thinking, you have failed miserably. Ditto if the colors you use to indicate something positive or something negative are in direct opposition to the way their culture views said colors. As the multiple examples in this chapter indicate, it's probably not possible to satisfy every single person every single time, which is why the research into what your audience's background is, what cultures they represent, and how to correctly appeal to them is so essential in getting things done right the first time.

2 Image credit: Khadija Bilal, "Here's Why It All Changed: Pink Used to Be a Boy's Color & Blue for Girls," *The Vintage News*, May 1, 2019, *https://oreil.ly/m5yC7*.

9

Common Pitfalls of Color Use in Data Storytelling

In addition to the cultural pitfalls that are mentioned in the last chapter, there are other obstacles and hazards you can encounter when dealing with color in data visualization. In this chapter, we'll go over some of the common problems that occur when you use data in storytelling as a cautionary tale to keep you from repeating the mistakes of the past.

Encoding Too Much Information or Irrelevant Information

A mistake we've talked about in this book is encoding too much information or irrelevant information. Color has its uses, but it is not necessary to use it for everything. Say you want to show how rapidly a specific region of the United States has grown popularity wise in the last 25 years. You could break up a map of the country into its various regions and use a different color on each, except that this would mean at least four to six different colors all on the same graphic, which would really distract your audience and give them way too much to look at.

A more palatable choice would be to highlight the region in question in a bright color and leave the rest of the country gray or in muted tones. You only want to showcase the positive impact of one part of the country, why give attention to the rest as well? There are simply too many different colors and too many that have a lot of similarity to one another. We need to use color to enhance figures and make them easier to read, not to muddle the data we are accenting by creating vast visual puzzles of colors, hues, gradients, and shades (Figure 9-1).

Figure 9-1. Filled map view demonstrating how color can be utilized to focus on a specific geographic region

Qualitative color scales are your best bet when there are between 3 and 5 categories that require color. Once you get up to the 8 to 10 set, you're starting to use colors that are not well known or that are very similar to one another, and thus are quite difficult to differentiate between. Maybe you can see the difference between blue-green and aqua when you have a shirt of each in your closet, but what about the person trying to figure out which is which from 30 feet away on a projection screen in a crowded conference room? Just as bad a decision is coloring for the sake of coloring, when there is no clear purpose in the use of the color. This also happens when we make the decision to color everything instead of just focusing on what needs to have color in it. It's gratuitous at best and winds up with our data presentations looking more like a rainbow than anything else.

We might try to differentiate between things by altering their saturation or hues, but that can be more confusing as it ends up making the colors indistinguishable from one another and any perceived meaning vanishes in the similarities.

Using Nonmonotonic Colors for Data Values

Colors need to indicate which values are larger or smaller than others, and the differences in colors need to visualize the differences between the values of the data. This fails to happen when designers use popular color scales that don't fill this need. The typical rainbow scale is a prime example of this, as it is effectively a circle where the colors at the beginning—the dark reds that bleed into orange and yellow—are the same as the colors at the end—the dark reds that evolve from purples and pinks. The scale starts out medium dark, then goes very light with orange, yellow, and green, then goes very dark with blue and purple, then goes back to medium dark again (Figure 9-2).

Figure 9-2. Full rainbow gradient view of saturated colors[1]

The stretch of light colors in the middle is just as much of a problem as the darkness at both ends. Because of this phenomenon, when all of these colors are used on a map, chart, or infographic at the same time, there's not clear discernment for the eye of the audience as to what's "bad" and what's "good." If you start at the far side of the rainbow scale and have those colors indicate the lowest levels of your points, with the far right side indicating the upper levels, you're going to get some very confusing results. Figure 9-3 shows us how the rainbow looks in grayscale mode. You can't really see the difference too much.

---

1 Image credit: "Rainbow Gradient Fully Saturated," Wikimedia Commons, *https://oreil.ly/jnYT7.*

rainbow scale

rainbow converted to grayscale

Figure 9-3. Two rainbow scales, one in full color and the other converted to grayscale[2]

Let's say we want to count the number of COVID-19 cases county by county in the state of Texas using the colors of a rainbow.[3] The average pair of eyes in the US that sees some countries lit up in red and others in pinks and greens are going to naturally assume that the red counties are the worst off, solely because of the connection between the color red and ideas of danger and negativity. Green and pink are more positive colors, and a look at them in certain counties would make most people think that those areas are relatively COVID free.

If you are going to do a data visualization that showcases something going from low to high or from less severe to more severe, you need to have the colors emulate that pattern. An easier solution would be to start with the lightest colors and graduate to the darkest. Use yellow, orange, and pink to indicate the counties where the count is fairly light, then dip into your reds and purples to show where trouble is brewing. The change from light to dark is one of the easiest for the human brain to follow, regardless of what country you are from. This is also an instance where not using any color at all is perfectly acceptable.

Another option is to have the map of Texas counties be gray throughout, except where cases are hitting at predetermined rates, say more than x cases per day. Then you could use two to three colors to set those counties off from the rest, such as yellow for counties with slightly higher ranges of cases per day, orange for those with even higher ranges per day, and red when the number of cases in the county is above another threshold per day (Figure 9-4).

That strategy would allow audience members to easily see what regions contain the highest concentrations of outbreaks overall, and then very quickly within that same graphic see where the densest outbreaks are occurring.

---

2 Image credit: Claus O. Wilke, *Fundamentals of Data Visualization*, O'Reilly, 2019.

3 "Texas COVID-19 Data," Texas Department of State Health Services, last updated November 7, 2022, *https://oreil.ly/IpLRk*.

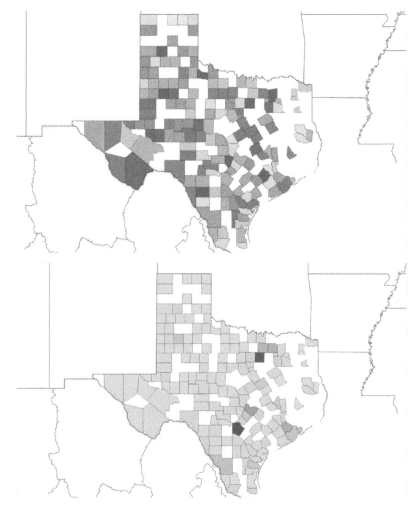

Figure 9-4. Geographical representation of Texas cities COVID cases with the top showing multiple colors and the bottom showing a more effective use of gradient colors

Failure to Design for Color Vision Deficiency

We dealt heavily with color vision deficiency in an earlier chapter, but a refresher course never hurt anyone. It can be so simple to hit on the red-and-green combination when we're dealing with data, especially if we are comparing something negative to something positive; it's practically our brain's go-to functionality. Eight percent of men having color blindness might not seem like a large amount until you consider that if 500 men are looking at your dashboard right now, 40 of them are not able to understand it if you haven't designed it properly.

In a world of 7.67 billion people, those numbers equate to 614 million men and 38 million women with some sort of color vision deficiency. Surely those numbers are large enough to make you want to try and produce work that's fit for everyone, right? Let's review a quick example (Figure 9-5).

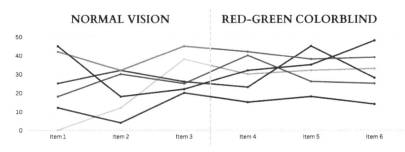

Figure 9-5. Multiple line graph that demonstrates normal vision (left) and red-green color blindness (right)[4]

This line graph demonstrates the difference between normal vision and the vision of someone with red-green color blindness. You can see how the lines on the right start to look very similar to each other, whereas they seem to be distinctly different on the left.

Side note: if these lines all look the same to you, then you might belong to the small group of individuals that have trouble with color vision.

Not Creating Associations with Color

If you're doing repetitive work for the same company, the worst thing to do is keep reinventing the wheel. If your color palettes work the first time, don't keep changing them! Focus on what works and start creating consistency and building a framework that your internal clients and external audience members can rely on when they see your work.

Just like the colors of a country's flag indicate a certain meaning to people when they see it over and over, so do the palettes that you employ for your design work. If blue works great for profits and orange means how many days the company has gone without an industrial accident, keep going back to the well on

---

4 Image credit: "Visualizing for the Color Blind," insightsoftware, July 14, 2022, *https://oreil.ly/TwDzg*.

them over and over again to build that friendly rapport in your audience's mind-set. Don't try to "spice things up" by using new colors every week.

Let's imagine that we normally presented our management team with a monthly report of profit by product subcategory. We use blue to demonstrate high profitability and orange to represent lower profitability. After a few months, we decided to color high profitability with purple instead. You can guess that there would be much confusion amongst the audience. Questions would be raised around the significance of the new colors (Figure 9-6).

Sub-Category	January	February	March	April
Accessories	2,245	1,558	2,316	1,825
Appliances	1,224	962	409	-377
Art	224	297	300	540
Binders	2,137	1,365	4,926	-865
Bookcases	-266	255	-429	-166
Chairs	1,739	629	1,856	1,184
Copiers	1,500		9,604	2,727
Envelopes	374	374	569	487
Fasteners	41	35	51	57
Furnishings	349	339	697	1,308
Labels	304	136	417	160
Machines	42	3,055	975	-553
Paper	1,080	1,484	2,666	1,700
Phones	1,567	1,475	2,588	2,850
Storage	1,309	499	1,706	1,058
Supplies	151	23	-852	2
Tables	-2,313	-1,129	-1,039	-1,557

Figure 9-6. Highlight table view that demonstrates the profitability of product subcategories across time

This is why consistency is key; once you find what works, stick with it.

When you keep changing colors, you have the audience trying to play a guessing game of what your intention is, if you've made a mistake, if you're just trying to be artsy, and so on and so forth. One color lets viewers immediately grasp increase and decrease in a specific metric, and do so in an authentic, serious way. You wouldn't want to show your board of directors how many people are leaving the company to work remotely in a line that changes from lime green to bright red to neon pink, would you?

Not Using Contrasting Colors to Contrast Information

Colors and numbers are much more similar than we think. Using contrasting colors on different forms of information allows your audience to make a very clear delineation between the two, even when the setup and style are completely the same. Say you're trying to show the percentage of US adults who say they use at least one social media site.[5]

If you have blue representing one age group, green representing another, pink one more, and purple showing off yet another, there is going to be a lot of head scratching involved from your audience. Not only do these colors not have a lot of difference between them, but they bleed into one another, making it hard to tell where one stops and the next begins without putting border marks on them, which is extraneous and unnecessary (Figure 9-7).

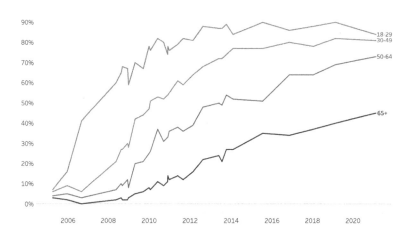

% of U.S. adults who say they use at least one social media site, by age

Figure 9-7. Line graph showing usage of social media across various age groups with colors that don't have much contrast

Your ambition is to show the contrast in information, so show it!

Take colors that complement each other like our old standbys blue and orange, or take one dark, cooler color and one light, warmer color to stand out against each other. If you need a third or fourth color, put them equidistant

---

5 "Social Media Fact Sheet," Pew Research Center, April 7, 2021, *https://oreil.ly/2dOes*.

between the first two so that none of them are too close to the other. Figure 9-8 shows us how we can improve the original line graph by using the rectangular color palette we learned about earlier in the book.

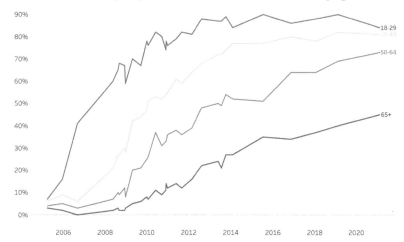

% of U.S. adults who say they use at least one social media site, by age

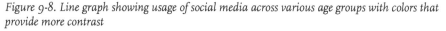

Figure 9-8. Line graph showing usage of social media across various age groups with colors that provide more contrast

Using contrasting colors becomes even more important when working with text within your visuals. You want your audience to be able to read your chart on their screen, even in low light. This becomes increasingly significant with smaller text. In addition to having a high contrast ratio, you should avoid complementary hues (e.g., red and green, orange and blue, etc.) and bright colors for backgrounds. Use this tool to test your color contrast, the brightness difference, and if colors are "compliant."

Figure 9-9 presents an example of contrast ratios; it shows where you have a safe choice, and where you are risking losing your audience.

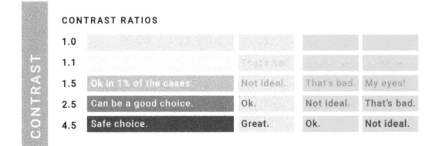

Figure 9-9. Contrast ratios of backgrounds and font colors[6]

Not Making the Important Information Stand Out

Your job as the data visualization designer is not to be fair and give every piece of data the same chance to be seen. Your job is to direct the audience's vision and attention to the specific story that you want to tell with this data. You are absolutely here to play favorites and to guide the audience through a very specific narrative to either inform them or convince them of a key point.

That means using a color that is a slam dunk when it comes to jumping off the page and getting lots of attention. Deep red, orange, yellow—they're all great choices, particularly when you mute or gray the less-important spots in your visualization.

In his visualization about malaria in Zambia (Figure 9-10), designer Daniel Caroli chose to highlight a single district in red to show how much it differs from the rest. Sinazongwe, a district located near bodies of water, has an extremely high rate of malaria cases compared to the other districts. The designer carries that message through his dashboard by applying color only for Sinazongwe while showing all other districts in gray for context.[7]

---

6 Image credit: Charlie Custer, "What to Consider When Choosing Colors for Data Visualization," Dataquest (blog), August 22, 2018, *https://oreil.ly/HGBQ6*.

7 Eva Murray, "The Importance of Color in Data Visualizations," *Forbes*, March 22, 2019, *https://oreil.ly/oUKus*.

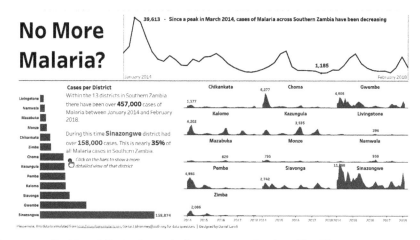

Figure 9-10. Dashboard illustrating malaria cases across Southern Zambia

You might have a certain affection for colors like eggplant, seafoam green, and lilac, but if the human eye can't tell the difference between those three and standard purple, green, and blue, you're going to run into trouble early and often. Remember that your purpose above all else is to make the information contained in the data as visually stimulating and clear as possible.

As beautiful as data can be, it's not an al fresco painting that should be open to interpretation from anyone who walks by its section of the museum. Make bold, smart color choices that leave no doubt what the purpose of the data is.

When you're dealing with "too much information" on one page, gray becomes your best friend. Take a look at the Figure 9-11, which shows before-and-after visualizations. We start with a line graph that shows us the quantity of products sold over time across various product subcategories. In the "before" image, you'll notice that it's difficult to glean any insights from the chart. There is simply too much going on. Once we decide to give our chart some focus, such as focusing on Binders only, we can re-create the chart to showcase the performance of that specific subcategory.

The use of gray for the remaining subcategories helps Binders to stand out, without losing the perspective of the performance of the other subcategories.

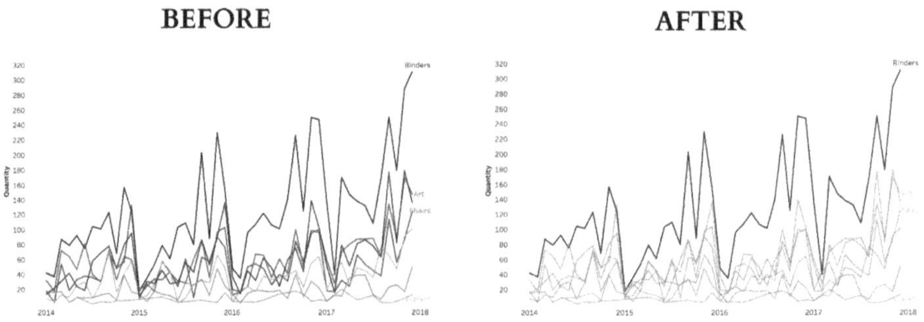

BEFORE   AFTER

Figure 9-11. Two multiple-line graphs demonstrating the power of using gray for supporting details and using a highlight color to alert our audience

Using Too Many Colors

Red, blue, and yellow? Great! Orange and purple and pink? Sure. Green and teal and aquamarine? Not so much. The human brain struggles when it has to process too many things at once. That's why you'll struggle to remember all the parts of the periodic table from high school chemistry, but you can remember all the words and dance moves to "Macarena" 30 years after it came out. Research says that seven is the maximum number of items that the brain can hold at one time—thus the reason many phone numbers are seven digits. The fewer the better. Remember: a lack of color often works just as well.

Let's say we are reviewing our top dozen customers (by largest amount of sales) and wanted to visualize these for our sales team. This way they'd have an idea of who is driving their sales portfolios. If we used a different color for each customer, it would start to look like the rainbow. This might look like a fun chart, but in truth, it is distracting to most. Our audience would sit and think about what the colors represent. If we look at the updated chart to the right in Figure 9-12, you'll notice that by simply moving away from using multiple colors and selecting a consistent color to represent all customers, we can easily digest the information and focus on what matters.

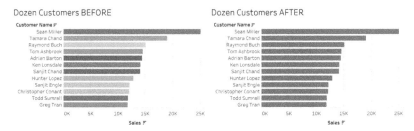

Figure 9-12. Two bar charts demonstrating customers with the most sales: the chart on the left uses too many colors while the chart on the right uses one to tell the story more effectively

Summary

Sometimes, fixing a color issue in a data visualization is as easy as removing most of the colors! Prior to finalizing a presentation, ask yourself: What do the colors represent in your chart? Are the colors necessary? Do they serve a purpose? Taking a moment to ponder these questions will help you decide if downsizing the number of colors makes sense.

Additional Examples

By now you have learned about color theory, color psychology, and how to avoid common pitfalls when working with colors in data visualizations and data stories. In this chapter, we'll tell some stories with data and demonstrate how color can help our audience understand the key insights. Let's go ahead and start our journey of data storytelling. We will review some different scenarios that will help you apply some of the concepts we've covered in the book.

Using Colors Found in Nature

What should we add to our salad menu? Let's imagine that we are working for a global restaurant chain that is focused on making salads. Those in charge of maintaining the restaurant menu asked you to find out which of these two ingredients they should add to their menu as a salad topping: oranges or grapes (Figure 10-1).

Figure 10-1. An orange and some purple grapes

To answer this question, we gathered data from Google Trends (*https://oreil.ly/GACnr*)—exploring and comparing the popularity of the search terms *orange* and *grape*.

Google Trends provides access to a largely unfiltered sample of actual search requests made to Google. It's anonymized (no one is personally identified), categorized (determining the topic for a search query), and aggregated (grouped together).

The data set provides us with a breakdown by region to demonstrate where these terms were searched for more frequently between the years 2017 and 2022, globally. Table 10-1 presents the raw data available for six countries along with the popularity of the search terms.

Table 10-1. Popularity of orange and grape for six countries

Country	Orange	Grape
Vietnam	29%	71%
Thailand	98%	2%
Portugal	84%	16%
Brazil	63%	37%
Greece	74%	26%
United States	57%	43%

If we were to put this data into a data visualization tool—in our case, we're using Tableau—our default settings would likely look like Figure 10-2.

Default Settings

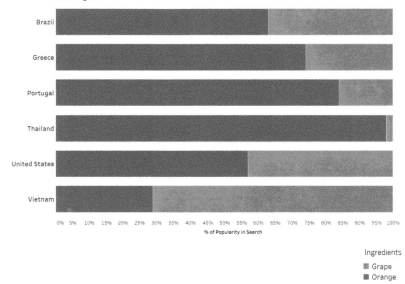

Figure 10-2. Stacked bar chart showing the popularity of ingredients by country using the default settings of Tableau, a data visualization tool

You'll notice that the default colors that were chosen for the ingredients are not very intuitive. Grapes were given the color orange and oranges were provided with the color blue. This is because our computers are simply not smart enough to identify these dimensions as fruit and therefore assign more intuitive colors to them. This actually might end up confusing everyone.

One great fact that we can leverage for our color selection here is that oranges tend to be the color orange, and grapes tend to be purple (unless you're thinking of green grapes). This helps us decide which colors to use in our data visualization.

Using a color picker tool (like in Canva), we can go back to Figure 10-1 and identify two good colors to use in our visualization. We identified the HEX value #ecb01d for oranges and the HEX value #9a8099 for grapes (Figure 10-3).

Figure 10-3. Oranges and grapes along with the HEX values for the key colors

Following is an updated data visualization that portrays the popularity of these ingredients in the six countries that we are focused on (Figure 10-4). We updated the colors to be more intuitive for the data we are working with and included labels on the bars to allow us to declutter and remove the color legend that we had initially. Additionally, we added a white divider line between the bars to provide another breakup of the two ingredients.

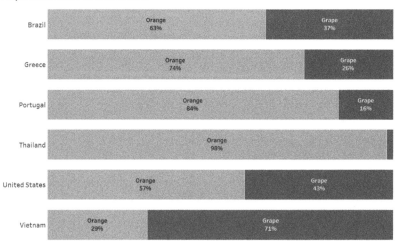

Figure 10-4. Bar chart showing ingredient popularity across countries with updated use of color

This insight can be taken into consideration when deciding which ingredients to add to restaurant menus across the world.

Using Color to Focus Your Audience

When you need to highlight an important item, a bright color can help it stand out. Gray is your best friend for the supporting data, or you can use a muted color for the "not as important" data points.

For example, take a look at the bar chart in Figure 10-5, which shows us the average number of air passengers by carrier name. If we wanted to focus in on JetBlue, we can color it blue and the rest of the bars light gray; this helps the audience focus on the specific bar.

This use of color immediately makes your audience focus on the blue line—it stands out from the rest of the bars.

Figure 10-5. Bar chart showing the average number of air passengers by carrier name, highlighting JetBlue Airways[1]

Another example of using brighter colors to draw the attention of your audience is displayed in Figure 10-6. The chart depicts product profitability by state and uses red to focus on the one unprofitable state across the country—Texas. The other states are colored with a neutral color, blue. The audience immediately

---

1 Image credit: "2021/W16: Monthly Air Passengers in America," data.world, last accessed November 7, 2022, https://oreil.ly/XJf65.

knows to focus in on Texas and will likely ask questions as to why this state has low profitability rates.

Profitability by State

Figure 10-6. Filled map view showing product profitability by state using the color red to focus on the one unprofitable state across the country: Texas

Designing for a Color Vision Deficiency Audience

If you know that there are members in your audience who have color vision deficiency or color blindness, you must take some extra steps to ensure that they will be able to effectively consume the information you present to them.

In this example, we are using a data set that highlights the relationship between the outdoor temperature and number of cricket chirps. There's a theory that you might be able to count cricket chirps to estimate temperature:[2]

temperature in degrees Fahrenheit = number of chirps in 15 seconds + 37

---

2 Peggy LeMone, "Measuring Temperature Using Crickets," *GLOBE Scientists' Blog*, October 5, 2007, *https://oreil.ly/NKUqq*.

Table 10-2 illustrates raw data that can be found on the pay-per-click expo website.[3]

Table 10-2. Relation of temperature, number of chirps, and number of crickets

Temperature (Fahrenheit)	Number of chirps (in 15 seconds)	Total crickets
57	18	2
28	20	5
64	21	10
65	23	15
68	27	6
71	30	8
74	34	10
77	39	15
20	10	10
24	8	8
25	7	7
58	5	2
71	2	10
74	14	5
77	30	7
20	34	8
24	26	3
25	16	4
58	8	2
71	12	1

Take a look at the chart in Figure 10-7 that demonstrates the relationship between air temperature and number of cricket chirps. The size of the circles is determined by the total number of crickets. The colors used here are green and red, with green depicting the majority of chirps and red being used to highlight three specific data points.

---

3 "5 Scatter Plot Examples to Get You Started with Data Visualization," PPCexpo, *https://oreil.ly/jmOK9*.

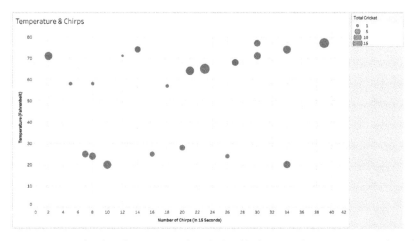

Figure 10-7. Scatter plot that demonstrates the relationship between air temperature and number of cricket chirps

If you do not have color blindness, you can probably identify the three red circles fairly easily. Figure 10-8, instead, displays them with numbers associated near them.

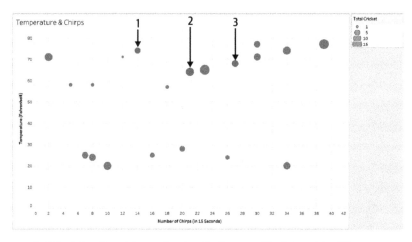

Figure 10-8. Adjusted scatter plot now showing the three specific data points of focus

We can use a tool called Coblis (*https://oreil.ly/bmKtk*), a color blindness simulator, which allows you to upload a photo and see how this visual would be seen by someone with color blindness. Can you still spot the red circles as quickly as you did the first time (Figure 10-9)?

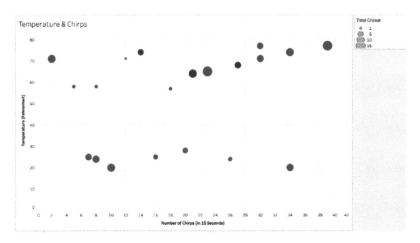

Figure 10-9. Scatter plot demonstrating the relationship between air temperature and number of cricket chirps as it would appear to someone with color blindness

Let's discuss an alternative to the visual that will be better suited for an audience that might experience color blindness.

Using the color gray for supporting data, and a bright blue for the three data points that we want to highlight, it becomes easier for our audience to distinguish between the circles in the scatter plot (Figure 10-10).

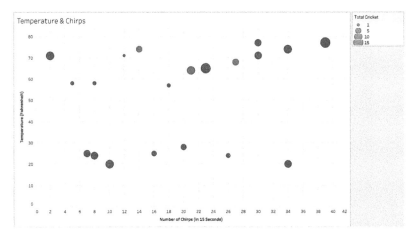

Figure 10-10. Previous scatter plot showing the three specific data points of focus now in blue and gray versus red and green

Now let's upload this image to our color blindness simulator to see the difference (Figure 10-11).

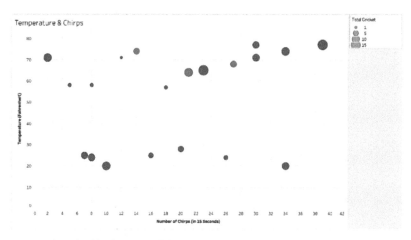

Figure 10-11. The color-blind version of the image with updated colors

You'll notice that there are hardly any differences between the two charts. This is great news! We have designed a visual that can be interpreted in the same way by our audience, even if they have trouble seeing different colors. This is also a better option for printing data visualizations in black and white (Figure 10-12).

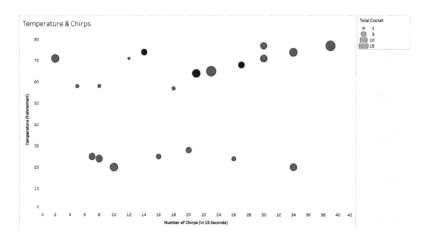

Figure 10-12. Previous scatter plot with updated colors in a grayscale mode view

The differences between the circles are still visible due to the darker shade of gray that is displayed.

Color Illusions

We discussed a few color illusions in the book, including the blue and gold dress, and the gray square that appears to change saturation when placed on a gradient background. Color illusions are images where surrounding colors trick the human eye into an incorrect interpretation of color. Let's review a few more examples of color illusions to consider when designing data visualizations.

All of the color illusions discussed here demonstrate how easy it is for the human eye to be "tricked" into seeing something that isn't there. This shows how important it is to be intentional with our use of color in data visualizations, and the colors used for our backgrounds.

ADELSON'S CHECKER SHADOW ILLUSION

Adelson's checker shadow illusion (published by Edward H. Adelson) depicts something hard to believe (Figure 10-13). The square marked B looks much lighter than square A, due to the "shadow" being cast upon it. However, the color on both squares is the same shade of gray. If you don't believe me, use any eye-dropper tool or print/cut the squares to verify that both square A and square B are precisely the same. I used a color picker in Canva to identify the HEX values for each square.

Figure 10-13. Adelson's checker shadow illusion[4]

---

4 Image credit: Jan Adamovic, "Color Illusions and Color Blind Tests," last accessed, November 7, 2022, *https://oreil.ly/ZtoVm.*

You can see the HEX values for both squares are exactly the same!

COLOR CUBE ILLUSION

Take a look at the squares marked A, B, and C in Figure 10-14. Can you believe that they all have the same color? Use any color picker, graphic program, or simply cover the remainder with your hand to see for yourself. You can even create a little telescope with your hand and look at each of the squares individually to see they are all the same color!

Figure 10-14. Colored cube on a black and white checkered background[5]

WHITE AND GRAY? MAYBE NOT!

When we look at the surface color of the A and B parts in Figure 10-15, they look different; one appears to be white and the other gray. However, they are exactly the same! Just use a finger to cover the place where both parts meet and you'll see.

---

5 Adamovic, "Color Illusions."

Figure 10-15. Two panels that appear to be different colors[6]

COLORFUL SPHERES (OR ARE THEY?)

A color contrast optical illusion makes it look like the balls in Figure 10-16 are different colors. In reality, they are all the same color and shading. I couldn't believe it at first, either—you can try to isolate each one by either using your hands to cover the image or looking really closely at the sphere in an isolated manner.

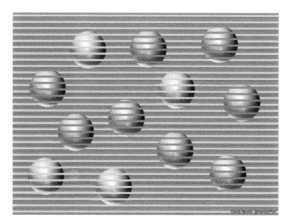

Figure 10-16. A dozen spheres with multicolored stripes that run over them[7]

---

6 Adamovic, "Color Illusions."

7 Image credit: Phil Plait, "Another Brain-Frying Optical Illusion: What Color Are These Spheres?" SYFY Wire, June 17, 2019, *https://oreil.ly/2bXLW*.

Figure 10-17 is the same image without the lines going across them to show you the difference.

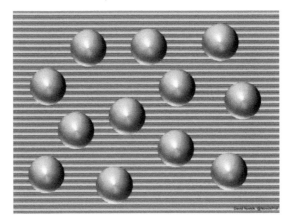

Figure 10-17. A dozen spheres on a multicolored striped background after removing the stripes from the spheres[8]

COLORFUL DOGS

Take a look at the two images of dogs in Figure 10-18: do they look different? They are the same! At first glance, one might look yellow and the other blue, but they are completely the same in color.

Figure 10-18. Image of the same-colored dogs on a diverging yellowish-green to blue background[9]

To make it clearer for you to view, we've taken the background away from the dogs. Do they look the same now (Figure 10-19)?

---

8 Image credit: Plait, "Another Brain-Frying Optical Illusion."

9 Image credit: Kyle Hill, "5 Optical Illusions That Show You Why Your Brain Messes with the Dress," Nerdist, February 28, 2015, *https://oreil.ly/kyfRo*.

Figure 10-19. Image of the same-colored dogs after removing the background[10]

They only looked different because of the gradient background.

It's important to keep these optical illusions in mind when designing your data visualization, as they can impact interpretation.

Summary

When designing data visualizations, it is important to use color intentionally. Leverage the immense power of color to help focus your audience's attention to specific insights.

---

10 Hill, "5 Optical Illusions That Show You Why Your Brain Messes with the Dress."

Conclusion

If you're seeing data points and hues, gradients, and degrees of saturation everywhere you look at this point, we're not surprised. There's a wealth of knowledge to take in when it comes to mastering color in data visualization, and for most people, it's a task they would rather trust to their computers than their own brainpower.

However, the default settings of your favorite graphics program are limited to appealing to the lowest common denominator or the default setting that highly-educated researchers carefully constructed in order to meet the needs of as many individuals as possible. While the default settings are a good place to start, as the designer of the data visualization, you have the knowledge and power to update the colors to create a more effective data story.

As data scientists, data analysts, and graphic designers, we have a responsibility to use color intentionally to convey key insights to our audience more effectively. This is no less than a combination of two great disciplines, the power of color and the power of data, coming together to tell stories, guide decisions, reveal facts, and dispel myths. It can be a massive responsibility that allows you to guide the future of your company, its targeted customers, even entire industries.

Great data visualization appears at the highest levels of industry—with its clarity, or lack thereof, defining the decisions of CEOs, boards of directors, and thousands of other executives, managers, and powerful people.

The proper use of color in data visualization helps people decide what to buy, what to wear, what to eat, what to believe in, and where to go. It gives government officials the information they need to decide what to vote on, what to fight for, and what to steer clear of. It is a remarkable fount of wisdom, source of knowledge, and defender of the truth.

When you approach a new data visualization project, treat it like it's your first day in the industry, starting with delving deep into the data itself to understand its point, power, and purpose, and don't take another step forward until you are completely confident in mastering exactly what the data is saying, who its audience is, and how you can best direct that message.

Once you have that knowledge firmly in place, set your sights on the intended audience that will receive the data, whether it be a single person or an entire company's base of customers. Make sure you know as much about this audience as possible: their age range, nationality, genders, cultures, anything that could possibly make a difference in how they perceive color and how they perceive information.

Know as much as you can about the colors that drive them and the colors that might offend them. Then get to work! Experiment with color complements, with a lack of color, and with various iterations that give you the best range of choices to present for approval or to run past your coworkers and fellow collaborators so that what gets sent on is the very best representation of the data, your company, and your own talents.

Helpful Resources

Here is a compilation of some helpful tools and resources that you can leverage on your data storytelling journey:

Color Thief (https://oreil.ly/CzIVB)
> Grab the color palette from an image using just JavaScript. Works in the browser and in Node. Just drag an image into your browser and you'll get a color palette, along with a dominant color.

Palette Generator (https://oreil.ly/QFMHd)
> Use the palette chooser to create a series of colors that are visually equidistant. This is useful for many data visualizations, such as pie charts, grouped bar charts, and maps.

Coolors (https://coolors.co)
> Generates color palettes with a tap of your space bar.

Viz Palette (https://oreil.ly/HNTLS)
> Shows you how the color palette will look on a dashboard with various charts and graphs, and allows you to view the dashboard with color-blindness filters, as well as grayscale mode.

i want hue (https://oreil.ly/i6UaF)
> Colors for data scientists. Generate and refine palettes of optimally distinct colors.

Canva Color Wheel (https://oreil.ly/G27nD)
> Helps you build a color palette for projects based on color theory, and then exports your palette for use in your design application or a Canva project.

Coblis (https://oreil.ly/bmKtk)
> Choose an image through the upload functionality or just drag and drop your image in the center of the Color Blindness Simulator.

Colormind (http://colormind.io)
> A color-scheme generator that uses deep learning. It can learn color styles from photographs, movies, and popular art.

Color Oracle (https://colororacle.org)
> A free color blindness simulator for Windows, Mac, and Linux. It takes the guesswork out of designing for color blindness by showing you what people with common color vision impairments will see in real time.

WebAIM (https://oreil.ly/po6BP)
> Offers an online contrast checker that shows the contrast difference between two colors to help you identify a color that meets the desired level of contrast.

Leonardo (https://leonardocolor.io/#)
> A one-of-a-kind tool for creating, managing, and sharing accessible color systems for UI design and data visualization.

ColorBrewer 2.0 (https://colorbrewer2.org)
> Allows users to create color schemes for maps and other graphics to show data that is readily readable. YOu can create maps using up to 12 different data classes, which can be sequential, divergent, or qualitative.

Adobe Color (https://oreil.ly/5kg8h)
> Allows users to create color palettes with the color wheel or image, and browse thousands of color combinations from the Adobe Color community.

Index

About the Author

Kate Strachnyi is the founder of DATAcated, providing brand amplification for data companies. Kate has delivered several courses and presentations on data storytelling, dashboard techniques, and visual best practices. Additionally, Kate is the host of the DATAcated Conference (which gathers thousands of data professionals) and the DATAcated On Air Podcast. Kate is on the DataIQ100 USA list for 2022. She was appointed a LinkedIn Top Voice of Data Science & Analytics in 2018 and 2019, and is also a LinkedIn Learning instructor.

She's also the founder of the DATAcated Circle, a community for ALL data professionals to engage in discussions. The Circle is also a hub to receive training / educational resources on data visualization best practices. She's the mother of two girls and enjoys running ultra-marathons and obstacle course races.

Colophon

The cover illustration is by Susan Thompson. The cover fonts are Gilroy Semibold and Bebas Neue Pro. The text fonts are Adobe Myriad Pro, Adobe Minion Pro, and Scala Pro, and the heading font is Benton Sans.

Printed in the USA
CPSIA information can be obtained
at www.ICGtesting.com
JSHW071416061123
51534JS00019B/163